Three Films of W. C. Fields

Faber Film

Woody Allen
Alan Bennett
John Boorman
Sergei Eisenstein
Peter Greenaway
Graham Greene
John Grierson
Trevor Griffiths
Christopher Hampton
David Hare
Derek Jarman
Neil Jordan
Krzysztof Kieślowski
Hanif Kureishi
Akira Kurosawa
Louis Malle
Harold Pinter
Dennis Potter
Satyajit Ray
Paul Schrader
Martin Scorsese
Andrey Tarkovsky
Robert Towne
Francois Truffaut
Andrzej Wajda
Wim Wenders

THREE FILMS OF

W. C. FIELDS

*

Never Give a Sucker an Even Break
Tillie and Gus
The Bank Dick

*

Introduction by
LOUISE BROOKS

faber and faber
LONDON · BOSTON

Never Give a Sucker an Even Break and *Tillie and Gus* first published
together in one volume in 1973
by Lorrimer Publishing Limited
The Bank Dick first published in 1973
by Lorrimer Publishing Limited
This collection first published in 1990
by Faber and Faber Limited
3 Queen Square London WC1N 3AU

Printed in Great Britain by
Clays Ltd, St Ives plc
All rights reserved

Never Give a Sucker an Even Break copyright 1941 by Universal City Studios Inc
Tillie and Gus copyright 1933 by Paramount Productions Inc
The Bank Dick copyright 1940 by Universal City Studios Inc
This edition © Faber and Faber Limited, 1990
Introduction © Estate of Louise Brooks, 1982, 1990
The Introduction was first published in Great Britain in
Lulu in Hollywood by Hamish Hamilton Ltd, 1982

A CIP record for this book is available from the British Library
ISBN 0-571-14385-7

CONTENTS

Acknowledgements   vi
Introduction by Louise Brooks   vii

NEVER GIVE A SUCKER AN EVEN BREAK
Credits and Cast   9
Never Give a Sucker an Even Break   11

TILLIE AND GUS
Credits and Cast   79
Tillie and Gus   80

THE BANK DICK
A Note on this Edition   125
Credits and Cast   126
The Bank Dick   127
Notes   195
Contemporary Reviews   208

ACKNOWLEDGEMENTS

Our thanks are due to Universal City Studios, Inc., for supplying dialogue continuities of *Tillie and Gus* and *Never Give a Sucker an Even Break* for the preparation of this volume, to Cinema International Corporation for making available a print of *Tillie and Gus*, and to Columbia Pictures Corporation, Ltd., for providing a print of *Never Give a Sucker an Even Break*.

INTRODUCTION
THE OTHER FACE OF W. C. FIELDS
Louise Brooks

Almost as cautiously as he won success in the theatre and films during the twenties, W. C. Fields won the hearts of American schoolboys during the sixties. A curious idol. For he had become their beloved not so much because they appreciated his comic art – based on the years of work he spent practising juggling and perfecting his timing, which is almost the whole of comedy – as because they imagined him to be a character like Quilp in Dickens' *The Old Curiosity Shop*. Quilp fell on the floor and rolled with laughter when he forced Sampson Brass to drink boiling rum and water. Fields was supposed to have pleasured himself by spiking Baby Leroy's milk with a possibly lethal dose of gin. It is the word 'work' that makes the schoolboys' love affair with Fields suspect. 'Work' was not a word in their vocabulary, and Fields was perhaps the only comedian known to them who revealed, through his stately procedures, the passionate amount of work he put into his performance.

In the sixties, many schoolboys wrote to me and came to see me. Most of them knew only my name and had never seen any of my films. They approached me with wildly uninformed flattery, after which, presuming me to be a forlorn old actress full of gratitude, they expected me to fill their arms with my most precious still pictures and sit three hours at the typewriter composing material that they could muck about, sign with their names, and present to the teachers of their film classes. Where Fields was concerned, it did not take me long to learn that these boys had seen few of his films, for in discussing any one of them they had great difficulty remembering its title or whether they had seen the whole of it or an excerpted reel or two. The Fields they idolized was the man they read about and superimposed on the Fields they saw (or didn't see) on the screen.

In 1778, Samuel Johnson wrote, 'Pointed axioms and acute replies fly loose about the world, and are assigned successively to those whom it may be the fashion to celebrate.' In 1922, when I first arrived in New York, I heard all sorts of gags, jokes, and anecdotes, and over the past twenty years of reading I have been brought to a condition of nausea as

I have found them 'assigned successively' to various film celebrities. There are two categories of celebrities – fitted with appropriate anecdotes – that writers and readers appear to dote on with foolish, untiring enthusiasm. They are the tramp-type woman star delineated by her outrageous conduct and the drunken actor whose cruel antics are considered hilarious. In the first category is the star who, in the favourite anecdote, goes into a smart restaurant clad only in a mink coat and a pair of slippers. Beneath the coat she is naked! The question is, how is it known – her nakedness? Does she take the coat off? In that case, the management would swiftly bundle her into a waiting cab, and every newspaper across the country would carry the story. Journalists refer to the mink-coat anecdote as a 'possible' item. It *could* happen. It probably has happened, but not to a star with the eyes of the press upon her. No documentation ever confirms this anecdote, which is usually assigned to some such star as Jean Harlow. Thomas Gray said, 'Men will believe anything at all provided they are under no obligation to believe it.' In the second category – the drunken actor, to whom are attached anecdotes out of the myths surrounding Irish wakes – writers have contrived an item so nearly impossible that no devoted reader about films doubts it for an instant. This *funny* story tells about a bunch of drunks who steal the body of an actor friend from his casket in a funeral home and set it up in a chair in another friend's house, during his absence. Surprise! I have consulted funeral directors and the police about this repulsive prank, and find that breaking into a funeral home would immediately arouse the forces of the law and get the pranksters clapped into jail. It is not necessary to add that such a frolic with the body of W. C. Fields would attract the notice of the press.

Where two or three are gathered together in his name, they do not waste time discussing W. C. Fields' films; they get right down to their 'favourite stories' about 'the little guy who looked life in the eye and told it where to go'. With more than fifty years separating them from the Fields of the theatre and his unseen early films, his admirers must rely on the word of journalists like Roger Doughty, who has written, 'Fields' characterization of a seedy, irascible, sharp-tongued drunk with a bulbous nose and an ice-cold heart made him a headliner in the *Ziegfeld Follies*, *George White's Scandals*, Earl Carroll's *Vanities* and such films as *Never Give a Sucker an Even Break* and *If I Had a Million* . . . In later years he jousted with Charlie McCarthy on Edgar Bergen's radio show.' The actual facts of Fields' character development are these: in

1923–24, he appeared on Broadway in the musical comedy *Poppy*. He played a small-time bungling cheat, an affectionate father with no trace of drunkenness. William LeBaron saw *Poppy*, and in 1925, after he had become head of production at Paramount's Long Island studio, he gave Fields a contract. *If I Had a Million* was released in 1932. Fields worked on Edgar Bergen's radio show in 1937 and 1938. *Never Give a Sucker an Even Break* was released in 1941. Another writer, Jim Harmon, quotes Bergen as saying, 'Fields would be drinking in the morning, drinking at noon, drinking in the afternoon. But he *never* acted as if he were drunk.' On his own, Harmon goes on to call Fields 'a man of monumental pettiness and eccentricity, with a hundred categories of hatreds and dislikes'. What, I wonder, is the source of this description, written in 1970? Bernard Sobel was the press agent of the *Ziegfeld Follies* for ten years. He covered most of Fields' appearances in that show, including his last, in 1925. At that time, Fields was a man of forty-six, completely formed as a comedian, completely set as a private person. Sobel, in his book *Broadway Heartbeat* (1953), writing about Fields' distorted biographies, says, 'Hollywood made him an autocrat whose odd behaviour was matched only by his drinking prowess. Somehow, I can't believe that Fields let fame distort him.'

No, it wasn't fame that distorted Fields. It was sickness and the clutching fear of being discarded to die on the Hollywood rubbish heap. If he must play a nasty old drunk and be publicized as a nasty old drunk in order to work on the Edgar Bergen radio show, then so be it. He was an isolated person. As a young man, he stretched out his hand to Beauty and Love and they thrust it away. Gradually he reduced reality to exclude all but his work, filling the gaps with alcohol whose dim eyes transformed the world into a distant view of harmless shadows. He was also a solitary person. Years of travelling alone around the world with his juggling act taught him the value of solitude and the release it gave his mind. He abhorred bars, nightclubs, parties, and other people's houses. He seems to have left no diaries, no letters, no serious autobiographical material. Most of his life will remain unknown. But, as Ruskin said, the history of no life is a jest.

The tragedy of film history is that it is fabricated, falsified, by the very people who make film history. It is understandable that in the early years of film production, when nobody believed there was going to be any film history, most film magazines and books printed trash, aimed only at fulfilling the public's wish to share a fairy-tale existence with its movie idols. But since about 1950 film has been established as an art, and its history recognized as a serious matter. Yet film celebrities continue to cast themselves as stock types – nice or naughty girls, good or bad boys – whom their chroniclers spray with a shower of anecdotes.

The most heartbreaking of all these books is Mack Sennett's *King of Comedy* (1954), taped and written by Cameron Shipp. Except in superficial observations, Sennett had not faith enough in his genius to risk a serious, luminous exposition of his world of comedy and the immortal grotesques who inhabited it. This world of universal laughter was silenced by its exclusion when the film corporations lengthened their feature films and filled out programmes with animated cartoons and newsreels. As a part of film history, as a person who was *there*, Sennett might have given readers the truth about the mysteriously manipulated scandals that destroyed two of his greatest stars – Mabel Normand and Fatty Arbuckle. But he so abused dates and facts that, for the most part, his anecdotes are historically worthless. What he had to say about Fields' salary and drinking habits is simply a footnote to his own vanity. Only one line in his book reminds me of the Mack Sennett I used to see in the Hollywood Roosevelt Hotel when I was living there, in 1936. Almost every day, from about noon, he would sit in the lobby for a couple of hours, smoking his cigars, watching the people go by. He was then only fifty-one – a big, healthy, wonderfully handsome and virile man. How could *he* have allowed himself to be discarded to die on the Hollywood rubbish heap? Although he spoke to no one, he was never bored. As he followed with keen and unembarrassed attention my flights in and out of the hotel, I wondered what thoughts lay behind the expressionless mask he wore in public. Now I know he was practising the art of paying attention. In his book, speaking of working for D. W. Griffith in New York, he says, 'I learned all I ever learned about making pictures by standing around watching people who knew how.' Anyone who has achieved excellence in any form knows that it comes as a result of ceaseless concentration. Paying attention.

I was in the *Ziegfeld Follies* with W. C. Fields in 1925. Bill adored beautiful girls, but few were invited to his dressing room. He was morbidly sensitive about the eczema that inflamed his nose and sometimes erupted on his hands, so that he had had to learn to juggle wearing gloves. After several devastating experiences with beautiful girls, he had decided to restrict himself to girlfriends who were less attractive, and whom he would not find adrift with saxophone players. Bill repeatedly entertained Peggy Fears and me with distinction. His bar was an open wardrobe trunk, fitted with shelves, which was planted, as if it were an *objet d'art*, beside his chair. While Shorty, the silent dwarf who was his valet and his assistant onstage, went about preparing our drinks, Peggy and I would dance around Bill, who sat at his make-up shelf listening to our nonsense with gracious attention.

I have never loved and laughed at W. C. Fields in films as I loved and laughed at him in the theatre. There are three reasons. First, in the theatre, he was a make-believe character playing in a make-believe world. In films, he was a real character acting in real stories. On the stage, the crafty idiocy with which he attempted to extricate himself from ludicrous situations was unbelievably funny. The same idiocy attending the same situations on the screen gave his 'real' character sometimes a degraded quality, often a cruel and destructive one.

Every night at the *Follies*, standing in the wings, I would watch Bill's 'Bedroom Sketch', with Edna Leedom, and his 'Picnic Sketch', with Ray Dooley. The 'Bedroom Sketch' opens in darkness. Bill and Edna are asleep in a double bed facing the audience. On Bill's side is a night table with a lamp on it; on Edna's side is a night table with a telephone on it. The telephone rings. Bill turns on the lamp and gets out of bed, sodden with sleep, his hair on end, wearing rumpled old white pyjamas. He trots round the bed on his little pink feet to answer the telephone. After mumbling a few words, he says, 'Good night, Elmer.' Then, looking down at Edna, who neither moves nor speaks, he adds, 'That was Elmer.' Bill turns out the light and gets back into bed. The telephone rings again. This time, when Bill says, 'That was Elmer,' Edna sits up in a fury. She is lovely. Her blonde hair is in perfect order and her lace nightgown exposes her lovely bosom and arms. Her anger does not hide the merriment in her eyes and the dimples in her cheeks. While they fight over the identity of Elmer, nobody in the audience is expected to believe that Edna is Bill's jealous wife. The film *International House* (1933) contains a bedroom sequence played by Bill in the same old white pyjamas, with another lovely blonde in an exquisite nightgown – Peggy Hopkins Joyce. But the realistic distaste with which she regards Bill spoils the fun.

In the *Follies*, Bill, as a father, played the 'Picnic Sketch' with Ray Dooley as his small daughter. At that time, Ray, although she was twenty-eight, with two children of her own, had the face of an infant monkey and a body that fitted nicely into a baby carriage. Her portrayals of obnoxious kids, aged from two to six, were brilliant travesties. She was not the aggressive child usual in theatre sketches. Up to the moment of an outburst, she was a passive child, following Bill's operations, her eyes glazed with anxiety. Making no sound, she watched him break in the door of an unoccupied house upon whose lawn was to be spread the litter of the picnic lunch. He burst into the house, outraged to find the door locked against honest, tax-paying Americans, and came out in triumph with a paper bag filled with stolen food. It was only after he opened a can of tomatoes with a hatchet, squirting the red juice in his face, that she set up the howls that made him flinch and recoil and yank his straw hat over his ears. As the traditional obnoxious kid, a little boy, Mickey Bennett, played Ray Dooley's part in the same picnic sequence in the film *It's the Old Army Game* (1926), in which I played the love interest. It was shot on the front lawn of the most lavish estate in Palm Beach – El Mirasol, the winter home of a J. P. Morgan partner, Edward Stotesbury. Not only was it a most improbable spot for a Fields picnic but what the production unit did to the lawn was frightful. During the five days of shooting, the litter converted it into a garbage dump; and when the trucks and forty pairs of feet finished their work, it looked like the abandoned site of an old soldiers' reunion.

My second reason for preferring Fields on the stage to Fields on the screen is that on the stage the audience saw all of him all the time. In 1925, when we were both working at Famous Players-Lasky's Long Island studio, I in *The American Venus* and he in *Sally of the Sawdust*, I would go to his set to watch him work. He paid no attention to camera setups. For each shot, he would rehearse the same business to exasperating perfection while his co-star, Carol Dempster, and the Director D. W. Griffith sat bored and limp in chairs beside the camera. Long shot, medium shot, two-shot, or close-up, Bill performed as if he were standing whole before an audience that could appreciate every detail of his costume and follow the dainty disposition of his hands and feet. Every time the camera drew closer, it cut off another piece of him and deprived him of some comic effect.

Having thousands of feet of close shots at his disposal, the film editor supplies my third reason for loving the stage Fields more than the film Fields. Fields never really left the theatre. As he ignored camera setups, he ignored the cutting room, and he could only curse the finished film, seeing his timing ruined by haphazard cuts.

William LeBaron, head of the New York Paramount Studio, was

responsible for attempting to divert Fields from fantasy to realism. Today, it is assumed that Fields was a big box-office star in the theatre and in films. He was not. The largest audience he attracted was the radio audience of 1937–38, which listened to his unedited dialogue with another creature of the imagination, Edgar Bergen's dummy Charlie McCarthy. But back in 1925 LeBaron believed that Fields could never achieve complete success without becoming a real person to the audience. After seeing Fields successfully play a character part in *Poppy*, LeBaron gave him a part in *Janice Meredith* (1924). When LeBaron moved to Paramount, he put Fields under contract. Between 1925 and 1938, LeBaron produced twenty-one Fields films. Yet it was after Fields escaped realism and returned to his world of make-believe that he made his best films. These were produced at Universal, between 1938 and 1941. This is a puzzling fact, considering that it was LeBaron who produced all the exhilarant Mae West fantasies at Paramount, managing to neutralize her schemes to portray a *real* femme fatale – or, as Fields put it, 'a plumber's idea of Cleopatra'.

The first of five Fields films directed by Eddie Sutherland was *It's the Old Army Game*. To shoot exteriors in February, 1926, Paramount sent the production unit to Ocala, an inland farming town in Florida. About six miles away was Silver Springs, which was advertised as having 'one hundred and fifty natural springs issuing from the porous Ocala limestone and flowing into a common basin'. The basin was filled with tropical fish, surrounded by tropical plants and flowers. This iridescent beauty was viewed from a glass-bottomed motorboat, which Eddie used for a love scene between William Gaxton and me. The citizens of Ocala, hoping to make Silver Springs a rich tourist attraction, welcomed our company as a means of publicizing their project. We were treated to so much Southern hospitality that the script got lost and the shooting schedule wandered out of sight. Nobody in Ocala seemed to have heard of Prohibition. And if ever there was a company that needed no help in the consumption of liquor it was ours. Eddie and Tom Geraghty (the writer) drank; William Gaxton, Blanche Ring, the crew, and I – everyone drank. Bill Fields, apart, drank his private stock with his girlfriend, Bessie Poole; his manager, Billy Grady; and his valet, Shorty. We were a week over schedule, and LeBaron was wiring to us 'All second cameraman's rushes tilted. What are you doing? Sober up and come home,' when Eddie decided that the picnic sequence absolutely must be shot on Mrs Stotesbury's lawn.

After a famous person dies, his biographers feel free to give him a glittering list of intimate friends. Anecdotes are so much tastier spiced with expensive names. Bill Fields' list grows with every telling. As far as I know, he had no intimate friends, and he loved only one person, whose name, Paul Jones, is meaningless to practically everyone. Paul Meredith Jones was born in 1897, in Bristol, Tennessee, a mountain village on the Kentucky border. In 1922, he turned up at the Paramount studio and got a job as a prop boy. In 1962, when he retired from that studio, he left behind one of the finest records as a comedy producer known to Hollywood history. He had produced comedies with Bing Crosby and Bob Hope; with Hope alone; with Martin and Lewis; with Jerry Lewis alone; with Danny Kaye; and with W. C. Fields. In 1931, while Paul was still an assistant director, LeBaron returned to Paramount and began to groom him as a comedy producer. Although LeBaron was tall and grey and elegant, and Paul was a small, sandy-haired hillbilly, they had much in common. Both were serene, witty observers of the scene rather than participants – warm and friendly, yet remote. Both were unpublicized, unknown in Hollywood society. But whereas LeBaron functioned above the storm, he could send Paul to any set where insecure comedians were fighting with insecure comedy directors and obtain peace.

Fields, Eddie, and I first knew Paul when he was the second assistant on *It's the Old Army Game*. His walk alone – the way he came on the set, as if he had ambled down the mountain to make a friendly call – was as soothing as a lullaby. Leaning on his cane, as relaxed as if he were leaning over a rail fence, his narrow eyes twinkling in his long, solemn face, he would listen to Bill and Eddie argue about the direction of a scene until they ran out of words. Then, with some easy, comforting remarks, he would make them feel just silly enough to laugh at themselves. When it came time to shoot the scene, the argument had settled itself – usually in Bill's favour. Paul became first assistant on *Tillie's Punctured Romance*. That is when he became Fields' confidant. They had a bond: women. Paul, too, adored beautiful girls who did not adore him. His handicap was his total distinctiveness. He did not look or act or talk like anyone else in Hollywood. Young girls were ashamed to go out with 'that little hillbilly'. He had fallen in love with a pretty extra girl, Doris Hill, and persuaded Eddie to give her a part in *Tillie*. During production, she met Monte Brice and married him.

The last time I saw Paul was in 1940, at his home. He had become a

powerful and wealthy producer without changing a bit. He was married to his pleasant secretary, Julia, and they were living in an old-
fashioned bungalow on an unfashionable street in Hollywood. I was
soon to leave Hollywood forever, and Paul's stories and imitations of
Bill Fields are the last happy memories I possess of that unhappy place.
Especially Bill's plot to get rid of Bessie Poole. Bessie was a large, plump
blonde who wore ruffled pink organdy dresses with matching hat,
gloves, shoes, and parasol. Her composure was indestructible. All Bill's
suggestions that she should leave him for her own good were deflected
with smiling contentment. Not being a cruel man or a brave one, he
designed a painless separation by means of a fictional business trip,
taking Paul with him to San Francisco. Bessie saw them off in Hollywood, waving goodbye, with her pink handkerchief, to Bill and Paul,
who were standing on the observation platform of the train. All the
time Bill was waving and beaming and calling goodbye to Bessie, he
was muttering his horrid plot into Paul's ear. When they arrived in San
Francisco, he would telephone his lawyer in Hollywood, instructing
him to present a generous check to Bessie and then stuff her on the first
train back to New York and the burlesque show she had come from.
Paul knew, of course, that Fields would never have the courage to carry
out the plot, which seemed so feasible as the train was pulling out and
he was calling, 'Goodbye, Bessie! Goodbye, my dear – my little
rosebud! Take care of yourself!'

NEVER GIVE A SUCKER AN EVEN BREAK

Never Give a Sucker an Even Break

CREDITS:

Directed by	Edward Cline
Production company	Universal
Screenplay	John T. Neville
	Prescott Chaplin
Original story	Otis Criblecoblis (W. C. Fields)
Photography	Charles Van Enger
Cameraman	Jerome Ash
Art direction	Jack Otterson
	Richard H. Riedel
Film Editor	Arthur Hilton
Musical director	Charles Previn
Musical score	Frank Skinner
Sound supervisor	Bernard B. Brown
Costumes	Vera West
Set decorations	R. A. Gausman
Associate director	Ralph Ceder
First assistant director	Howard Christie
Assistant to Ralph Ceder	Melville Shyer
Running time	70 minutes
First shown	1941

CAST:

The Great Man	W. C. Fields
His niece	Gloria Jean
His rival	Leon Errol
Butch	Billy Lenhart
Buddy	Kenneth Brown
Mrs Hemogloben	Margaret Dumont
Ouliotta Hemogloben	Susan Miller
The producer	Franklin Pangborn
The producer's wife	Mona Barrie
Peter Carson, a young engineer	Charles Lang
Madame Gorgeous	Anne Nagel
The salesgirl	Nell O'Day
The soda jerk	Irving Bacon
The waitress	Jody Gilbert
The cleaning woman	Minerva Urecal
The engineer	Emmett Vogan
Receptionist	Carlotta Monti

NEVER GIVE A SUCKER AN EVEN BREAK

We know that we are in a picture within a picture when we open on a large sign: ESOTERIC PICTURES WEST COAST STUDIO.

Now we dissolve to a view of the studio from outside the main gate, basking in the Californian sun, before another dissolve takes us to the drive within the studio. Buses are waiting for the extras, who are proving they are not spare by hurrying about. A clown comes on to herald GORGEOUS, a handsome woman, who goes over to chat to CHUCK, a bus driver.

GORGEOUS: *Hi ya, Chuck.*

By the bus now, GORGEOUS talks to CHUCK.

CHUCK: *Hello, Gorgeous. Oh say, your daughter's looking for you.*

GORGEOUS: *Oh thanks, I'll take the next bus.*

CHUCK: *O.K., Gorgeous.*

In a side street now, GLORIA JEAN is seen pumping up her bicycle tyre to music. She is rather glamorous for a moppet, but this is Hollywood. She sees GORGEOUS coming over.

GLORIA: *Hello, Mother. Who are you doubling today?*

GORGEOUS: *Lydia Flickman in an aerial act.*

GLORIA: *Be careful!*

GORGEOUS: *Say, I though you were supposed to be rehearsing.*

Now we track along the street with GLORIA and GORGEOUS as they walk along, leaving the bicycle.

GLORIA: *Haven't even started yet.*

GORGEOUS: *Well, you knock 'em over in that rehearsal and I'll let you support me.*

GLORIA: *Uncle Bill said if he sells his script you won't have to work any more.*

GORGEOUS: *Your Uncle Bill is too good. We owe him too much already.*

GLORIA stops and opens her bag. We are closer now to see her take out a horseshoe and spit on it for luck.

GLORIA: *Look what I found this morning.*

11

Closer again, we watch GORGEOUS also spitting on the horse-shoe.

GLORIA: *Close your eyes. Wish!*

Both the ladies now close their eyes and GLORIA throws the horseshoe over her shoulder. Behind them, the crash of breaking glass. They run for it.

At the end of a narrow building, a pile of water-bottles falls breaks, and we dissolve to another sign, this time a billboard advertising:

W. C. FIELDS

in

'The Bank Dick'

The Great Man FIELDS himself poses in front of the billboard, looking at his fame. We move back to show two boys, BUTCH and BUDDY, on the sidewalk, carrying musical instruments. They stop and look at the billboard.

BUDDY: *Was that a buptkie!*

Now we are close on the angry FIELDS himself.

W. C. FIELDS: *You're about to fall heir to a kitten's stocking.*

Back on BUTCH and BUDDY, looking off.

BUTCH: *What's a kitten's stocking?*

FIELDS is ready for action.

W. C. FIELDS: *A sock on the puss.*

The boys leave in disgust.

BUDDY: *Another buptkie!*

FIELDS looks round in baffled fury.

VENDOR off: *Raspberries!*

Back on the billboard of 'The Bank Dick'.

VENDOR off: *Raspberries!*

FIELDS' fury is mounting as he looks off to see the VENDOR drive by the billboard in an ancient Ford, selling his berries.

VENDOR: *Raspberries!*

But the near wheel of his jalopy is punctured. With a hiss, the tyre goes soft.

VENDOR off: *Raspberries!*

FIELDS almost begins to grin, or is it a snarl?

VENDOR off: *Raspberries!*

A MAN and a GIRL now come on as the Great Man stands in front of his billboard of 'The Bank Dick'. The man stops,

12

but the GIRL goes on and walks in front of FIELDS, before looking back past him.

Now close to FIELDS, we see him giving the GIRL the eye as he removes his straw hat, awfully gallant.

W. C. FIELDS : *How are you, Tootie-pie? Everything under control?*

GIRL : *Why . . . who are you talking to?*

The MAN comes on and jerks FIELDS around. Now further away, we see the MAN knocking FIELDS down under the billboard. The GIRL stands by, then goes off with the MAN.

FIELDS pulls himself up by the fence and grumbles to himself.

W. C. FIELDS : *All five of 'em hit me at once.*

Now FIELDS rises over the back of the fence and lumbers onto the sidewalk. WOLFE comes on and startles him.

WOLFE : *Hi!*

FIELDS runs his hand through his straw hat, so that it circles his arm. He cannot get the hat off.

WOLFE talks to FIELDS by the billboard, as FIELDS slowly works out how to get the straw brim off his arm.

W. C. FIELDS : *Ha! It's a lucky thing I recognised you. I thought it was that guy coming back. I was about to clout your brains out.*

WOLFE : *How about a part in this new picture you're going to do?*

W. C. FIELDS : *Go away or I'll kill you. You're all right . . . you're all set.*

WOLFE beams with gratitude.

WOLFE : *Thank you, Mr Fields.*

FIELDS is his old expansive self, goose of the walk.

W. C. FIELDS : *How'd you like to hide the egg and gurgitate a few saucers of Mocha Java?*

WOLFE : *No thanks. I've just had breakfast.*

W. C. FIELDS : *Very well . . . very well. Call me up at . . . sometime . . . at the house.*

WOLFE : *What time?*

W. C. FIELDS : *Oh, couple o'clocks.*

Dissolve to outside a bright restaurant, where men are dashing in for a quick bite out of the traffic. Then dissolve to inside the restaurant, where a large WAITRESS is smoking and reading a paper, back of the counter. FIELDS comes in,

13

whistling.

W. C. Fields: *Ah, good morning, Beautiful.*

The Waitress goes on smoking and holding her paper as she sneers.

W. C. Fields off: *What do you hear from Garcia?*

Now Fields is tossing his lidless hat at the hat rack. The hat settles down on top of the hat rack, but as it has no top, it slides down the column of the rack, and we tilt down with it to show it landing on the floor.

W. C. Fields off: *Ah . . .*

Fields sits down at a table near us, watching his hat.

W. C. Fields: *Ringer! Got a menu?*

The Waitress does not like leaving her two other customers at the counter, nor her paper, nor her smoke. We track with her to the end of the counter, where she edges through the opening.

Fields waits for her to come over, but she only comes close enough to throw the menu to him.

W. C. Fields: *Thank you. Thank you. Aaah!*

Fields considers the festive card while the Waitress stands by him.

W. C. Fields: *Is there any goulash on this menu?*

The Waitress wipes a stain off the card with her apron.

Waitress: *That's roast beef gravy.*

W. C. Fields: *Ah! Roast beef gravy . . .* Begins to mutter . . . *Is that steak New York cut? What about . . .*

As Fields mutters on, the Waitress crosses off the items one by one on the menu card. Then she begins putting ice water into her customer's glass.

In close-up, we see the ice and water being poured into the glass and overflowing.

At the table, Fields shrinks back as the Waitress slops the ice water over him. He sadly removes ice cubes from within his clothes.

The Waitress dumps the pitcher on the counter.

W. C. Fields off: *No extra charge for the cold shower, I hope.*

The Great Man tries hopefully again.

W. C. Fields: *Do you think it's too hot for pork chops?*

Back at his table, the Waitress crosses the chops off the

14

menu, while the seated FIELDS watches her cancelling most of the rest of the card.

W. C. FIELDS: *Ah! That practically eliminates everything but ham and eggs* . . . Setting his glass aside . . . *Forgot about that. Er* . . . *no ham? Two fomented eggs in a glass*

WAITRESS: *Cup.*

W. C. FIELDS: *Uh* . . . *yes* . . . *cup. And some whole wheat* . . .

WAITRESS: *White.*

W. C. FIELDS: *Yeah* . . . *some white bread. Yes. And a* . . . Swats at a fly . . . *Get away from there* . . . *And a cup of Mocha Java with cream.*

WAITRESS: *Milk.*

W. C. FIELDS: *Uh* . . . *milk. Yes. That's fine.*

WAITRESS: *Two in the water* . . . *Easy.*

W. C. FIELDS: *I don't know why* . . .

The WAITRESS now goes back to the counter with the other two customers. She looks back as FIELDS grumbles on.

W. C. FIELDS off: . . . *I ever come in here. The flies get the best of everything.*

Back to FIELDS, as he scrapes a cemetery of flies off the table.

W. C. FIELDS: *Oh, go away* . . . *go away!*

Dissolve to the exterior of Stage 6 at the Studio. There is Spanish music and GLORIA JEAN's voice singing 'Estrellita'. Now we see GLORIA JEAN in Spanish costume and in close-up, as she sings a Spanish song.

GLORIA: *Que miras mi dolor*
    Que sabes me sufrir
    Baja y dime se me quieres un poco
    Porque yo no puedo sin su amor vivir
    Estrellita del lejano cielo
    Que miras mi dolor
    Que sabes me sufrir
    Baja y dime se me quieres un poco
    Porque yo no puedo sin su amor vivir
    Tu eres . . . [1]

---

[1] This Hispanic ditty was subtitled as follows:
    Though a million twinkling stars are shining
    I watch for one alone

Just as well that Uncle Bill was off the set, really . . .

As GLORIA JEAN sings and rises, we track back to show her with gypsies seated round a fire. They also rise as she walks forward. The track continues back past a camera unit on a crane, which elevates and moves back with GLORIA. We also see the mike boom on a dolly with its operators, electricians with their various lights, a script girl and assistant directors. Now the overhead lights are brought into the scene, and people in canvas seats move their chairs out of the way of the mike boom. GLORIA now heads back for the fire, and the whole action of the gypsies and the studio people is put into an exact reverse, as if played backwards.

Now we cut to a medium close shot of the stage, where operators man the mike boom and track back across the stage, the camera unit moving with them. The assistants listen hopefully.

GLORIA off : *Estrella mi faro de amor . . .* [1]

Now we follow the camera on its crane as it shoots the scene.

GLORIA off : *. . . Tu sabes que pronto . . .* [2]

Now we are with the sound mixer in front of his mixing panel, as he listens through his ear-phones and makes adjustments.

GLORIA off : *. . . he de morir . . .* [3]

Now we see two sheep in close-up by a bush, one looking off.

GLORIA off : *Baja y dime . . .* [4]

A donkey's head is now seen, as it listens.

GLORIA off : *. . . si me quieres . . .* [4]

The seated script girl and her assistant also listen and make notes.

Oh, little star of love
Shine upon my heart's unrest with trainquil light
Rise, star of Beauty
Quench my ardent thirst for love tonight
Though a million twinkling stars were falling
Their fires I'd never miss
If one fair star I loved
Shining on like my desire
With deathless flame
Evermore should flood my darkness
With tender gladsome ray
Oooh . . .

16

GLORIA off : . . . *un poco* . . . [4]

Back now to the studio woods with the gypsies following the
singing GLORIA JEAN, and the mike boom on the dolly following them, and the camera also following until GLORIA stops
and turns round by the fire, so that the camera can move
into a close-up on her, while the gypsies fade away, allowing
the scene to end as it began, with GLORIA JEAN trilling in
close-up.

GLORIA : . . . *Porque yo no puedo*
Sin su amor vivir.[5]

A pair of hands comes onto the screen with the slate reading :

Esoteric Pictures, Inc

Director JOHNSON

Cameraman CHRISTIE

Date Nov 17

Test

GLORIA JEAN (in chalk)

JOHNSON and the script girl are now featured in the bustle on
the set, as JOHNSON talks on the telephone.

JOHNSON : *Oh yes, Mr Pangborn.*

Now we are in close-up.

JOHNSON : *Yes. We just made it. Huh? Yes. I'll have Gloria Jean
ready whenever you say. All right. Thank you, Mr Pangborn.*

Dissolve back to the restaurant, where FIELDS is seated at his
table, munching the ruins of his meal, with the WAITRESS
back of the counter gabbing at him.

WAITRESS : . . . *And another thing. You're always squawking
about something. If it ain't the steak, it's something else.*

FIELDS answers back, ruminating on his food.

---

[1] The mistitling continues :   *Oh, my little star*
                                    So high, so far . . .
[2] And :   *If I only knew . . .*
[3] And :   *How to climb to you . . .*
[4] All together, these mellifluous snippets are titled :
                                    I'm yearning . . .
                                    For your light, my little star
[5] The final debacle reads : *Shine upon me from your heights afar/My little
star of love.*

W. C. Fields: *I didn't squawk about the steak, dear. I merely said I didn't see that old horse that used to be tethered outside here.*

The Waitress is angry as she watches.

Waitress: *You're as funny as a cry for help.*

Now we see the seated Fields finishing up his meal as the Waitress leaves the back of the counter and goes over to him.

Waitress: *You also pulled that old gag about breaking your fork in the gravy.*

W. C. Fields: *I didn't say anything about breaking the fork in the gravy. Usen't you to be an old Follies girl?*

Waitress: *You know . . . There's something awfully big about you.*

W. C. Fields pleased: *Thank you, dear.*

Waitress: *Your nose.*

W. C. Fields looking at her rear end: *Something awfully big about you, too.*

Over at the door, a Man comes in. We track with him to the counter, where he and the Waitress volley a quip or two at each other.

Man: *Hiya, Tiny!*

Waitress: *Hiya, Joe!*

She moves back of the counter to serve him.

Man: *Give us a cup of Jarno.*

Now the Great Man is seen very close, as he wipes his grumbling lips exactly with his napkin.

W. C. Fields: *Probably means Mocha Java.*

Fields arises with majesty and approaches the Waitress.

W. C. Fields: *Er . . . what's the amount of the insult?*

Waitress: *That'll be thirty-five cents.*

At the end of the counter, Fields pays the Waitress.

W. C. Fields: *Thank you. Have you any imported cigars?*

The Waitress holds out a box at him.

Waitress: *Stingaroos . . . Four for a nickel.*

Fields carefully selects four of the stingaroos.

W. C. Fields: *Oh, that's fine. As long as they're imported. If an old friend of mine ever comes in here and gives you a ten dollar tip . . . scrutinise it carefully . . . cause there's a lot of counterfeit money going around. I'll give you the nickel. There.*

Waitress: *If I get any counterfeit nickels or pennies, I'll know where they came from.* FIELDS *chuckles evilly.* You're so clever.

She rings up the cash register.

W. C. FIELDS : *Who told you I was clever?*

WAITRESS : *All your friends at the studio told me.*

W. C. FIELDS : *Oh drat . . . I told them not to tell you.*

His hands seem to be juggling pretty near her.

WAITRESS : *And another thing . . .*

Close on her complaint.

WAITRESS : *. . . Don't be so free with your hands.*

FIELDS holds out his cigars, showing his hands are full.

W. C. FIELDS : *Listen, honey, I was only trying to guess your weight . . . you take things too seriously.*

The WAITRESS does not believe a word of it.

WAITRESS : *Baloney, maloney, malarkey . . . you big Kabloona.*

FIELDS starts to get away from the end of the counter.

W. C. FIELDS : *Kabloona . . . I haven't been called that for two days.*

At the other end of the counter, a couple sit, while the tables are quite full with people eating. As FIELDS moves across to the hatstand, he overhears a MAN talking.

MAN : *I suffered from high blood pressure for years . . . then I lost my dough and had to give it up.*

W. C. FIELDS : *Very comical.*

As he moves across to the hatstand, we track with him and watch him picking up his lidless straw hat and running it up the central column. A closer shot shows FIELDS looking round furtively, with the MAN at the table watching him. FIELDS leaves his own hat and takes a panama and puts it on. We track back with FIELDS as he makes his jaunty way back across the restaurant until the WAITRESS stops him.

WAITRESS : *Aren't you a little confused?*

W. C. FIELDS : *Eh . . . which way?*

WAITRESS : *Your hat.*

W. C. FIELDS : *Oh, thanks a thousand times. Yes . . . I mistook it. Thank you. Excuse me, blimpie-pie.*

He takes off the panama and replaces it with his own lidless hat, which he has to put on. We track with him as he moves off. The WAITRESS and the other customers stare at the Great Man and petty thief. As FIELDS passes JOE at the

19

counter reading the paper, he strikes a match on JOE's pants and lights one of the cheap cigars to prove his nonchalance. Close now, we see the cigar is still wrapped in cellophane, which catches on fire and startles FIELDS.

W. C. FIELDS : *Oh . . . ho . . . I forgot to take the cellophane off. Very fortunate it didn't burn my hat.*

He removes the cellophane and leaves the restaurant. Behind him, the WAITRESS watches, shaking her head.

Dissolve to a medium shot outside Stage 6, where MR PANGBORN avoids a man passing on a bicycle and opens the door leading onto the stage.

Men are setting up the next shot on the stage as MR PANGBORN comes in, and we track with him past a wind machine, two men practising a German goose-step, and people shouting for the hell of it, until he reaches the end of the stage, where GLORIA JEAN, BUTCH and BUDDY are rehearsing near a piano, where a PIANIST is playing.

GLORIA : *With a hot cha cha and boop boop de doop/And a scaddily daddily dinky doo . . .*

Close by the piano, the three rehearse, with the studio noise all about them.

GLORIA : *You can dig dig dig/When you cut a rug/When you waddily daddily doodle with me . . .*

In a large close-up, GLORIA sings on.

GLORIA : *With a hot cha chá and a boop boop de boop . . .*

In the close-up, the laughing BUTCH plays his bull-fiddle.

GLORIA off : *You can dig dig dig/When you cut a rug . . .*

In close-up, BUDDY plays his accordion and stares off.

GLORIA off : *When you waddily daddily doodle with me.*

Now we close to MR PANGBORN, yelling to make himself heard above all the noise, while his assistant director JOHNSON blows a whistle beside him.

MR PANGBORN : *Quiet! Quiet!*

JOHNSON : *Quiet!*

The noise stops. On the stage, the carpenters and prop men stand and stare.

MR PANGBORN strides forward with JOHNSON and the construction FOREMAN.

MR PANGBORN : *All right, Gloria Jean . . . we'll rehearse the number.*

FOREMAN : *You know we have to get this set finished by morning?*

MR PANGBORN : *Well . . . what am I supposed to do?*

FOREMAN : *Let my men continue working.*

JOHNSON : *They only have to stop working when we rehearse. I'll give you one whistle for quiet and two whistles they can resume work. Is that O.K., Mr Pangborn?*

MR PANGBORN : *Well . . . er . . .*

In a group, we now see GLORIA and the two boys by the PIANIST, with MR PANGBORN and his hovering aides nearby. JOHNSON blows his whistle and the carpenters start to work. MR PANGBORN now approaches GLORIA and yells.

MR PANGBORN : *Quiet!*

The whistle shrills again and all stop work. MR PANGBORN looks through GLORIA'S sheet music.

MR PANGBORN : *This . . . this is the song that you are to sing . . .*

GLORIA : *But this is the song Uncle Bill told me to sing.*

MR PANGBORN : *Uncle who?*

GLORIA : *Mr Fields.*

MR PANGBORN : *Swish swash . . . this is the number that you are . . .*

BUTCH is by JOHNSON with the FOREMAN and his men watching.

MR PANGBORN off : *. . . to sing.*

BUTCH blows the whistle.

FOREMAN : All right. Go on.

All start hammering and working.

MR PANGBORN is furious, as he stands by GLORIA and the PIANIST.

MR PANGBORN : *Quiet!*

As BUTCH smirks, JOHNSON blows his whistle. The FOREMAN is furious, as his men stop working.

JOHNSON : *Quiet!*

MR PANGBORN is rather uncertain by the side of GLORIA.

MR PANGBORN : *Er . . . Johnson . . .*

As the workmen all stand around watching the group at the piano, MR PANGBORN goes up to JOHNSON, trailing the music sheets which unfold behind him

MR PANGBORN : *Why do I have to work on a stage as busy as this with forty-eight stages in the studio?*

JOHNSON : *I'm sorry, Mr Pangborn, but they're all busy.*

MR PANGBORN : *Busy?*

GLORIA is standing by the PIANIST on his stool.

GLORIA : *I don't like this song.*

PIANIST : *Neither do I, Gloria. Come on, we might as well let him have it.*

We see the PIANIST start to play. GLORIA parks her gum on the piano and starts to sing a cadenza.

GLORIA : *I hear a song so gay . . .*

By JOHNSON, his assistant director, MR PANGBORN looks at the music and begins to fold it up, as GLORIA trills away. She nightingales along, the cadenzas flying, seen with the PIANIST and in close up.

GLORIA : *I hear it all the day/I hear it bring/A message of spring . . .*

The workmen are standing by, watching MR PANGBORN and JOHNSON fold up the music. As the two of them move past the FOREMAN to the piano, we track ahead with GLORIA trilling off and on.

GLORIA : *Birds and flowers,*
 Lovely bowers . . . Ah . . .
 Greet the sun on high
 Night and day . . . A-a-a-ah
 Breezes play . . . A-a-a-ah
 Gently . . . A-a-a-a-a-ah.

GLORIA carols her final cadenza in close-up.

JOHNSON blows his whistle.

FOREMAN : *All right!*

As the workmen thump and bang on their jobs again, the furious MR PANGBORN grabs the whistle and blows it.

JOHNSON : *Quiet!*

MR PANGBORN moves to talk to GLORIA and the PIANIST, with the workmen suspended like statues behind him.

MR PANGBORN : *No, no, no, Gloria Jean. I want more life!*

He puts his hand on GLORIA's parked gum.

Now we see BUDDY chewing gum, while BUTCH spits out a cherry pip. GLORIA and the PIANIST give a start as the cherry pip hits Mr Pangborn, and he looks round for the culprit. He sees the two boys, the Foreman and two workmen staring back at him, their jaws unmoving.

He feels the back of his neck and looks off, suspicious and angry.

The two boys and the Foreman look back. The music begins again.

Mr Pangborn takes his hand from the back of his neck and wipes it. Gloria begins to sing again.

Gloria: *Gaily through the swaying trees/Darting sunbeams light the forest . . .*

The Foreman still watches, as Butch and Buddy begin to eat cherries again.

Gloria off: *While the zephyrs kiss the murmuring leaves . . .*

Butch and Buddy fire out a volley of cherry pips.

Gloria off: *Sweetly fragrant . . .*

Mr Pangborn jerks as the pips hit him on the back of his neck. He glares and looks round.

Gloria off: *. . . with the breath . . .*

Butch and Buddy sit and look off, while Gloria trills a cadenza. The furious Mr Pangborn looks back again at Gloria.

Gloria: *. . . of Spring.*

The Foreman, the workmen and Johnson watch Mr Pangborn conducting as Gloria sings and the piano plays. Two extras march on doing the goose-step past Gloria, with their Instructor following them, raving.

Gloria: *A-a-a-a-ah!*
> *High in the sky above*
> *Birds are winging*
> *Loudly singing*
> *And the chorus that they sing . . .*

Instructor: *No, no! How many times do I have to tell you . . .*

We cut back to Butch and Buddy eating their cherries again. Butch offers cherries to the Foreman, who is standing by. He takes some and eats them.

Instructor off: *It's one, two three, four! How many times do I have to tell you? One . . .*

Gloria off: *. . . It's a welcome again to Spring.*

23

The Foreman slowly munches his cherries.

Gloria off: *A-a-a-ah!*

Butch munches and watches.

Gloria off: *A-a-a-ah! Ah-ah! Ah-ah!*

Mr Pangborn beats time, very pleased, as Gloria trills out more cadenzas.

Butch spits out a cherry pip.

Mr Pangborn gets it on the back of the neck as he beats time. He whips round.

The Foreman is now spitting out a cherry pip.

The furious Mr Pangborn now rushes off, and comes in by the Foreman and the two boys eating their cherries. He pulls the Foreman's nose, and the Foreman pulls his nose.

Gloria off: *Love fills the air*
　　　　A-a-a-ah!

The workmen watch Mr Pangborn fighting the Foreman. The two boys are delighted. Two male dancers skip on, practising a routine. By mistake, Mr Pangborn hooks onto the arm of one of them. We pan with him as the two men dance away with him, until he shakes himself free. Pan back with him as he returns to glare at the Foreman, before moving off, flicking his fingers.

Gloria off: *Love's everywhere . . ./Every lover is . . .*

Gloria trills on in close-up.

Gloria: *Sighing of love undying . . .*

In front of the seated workmen, Mr Pangborn tries to direct Gloria Jean. The music stops.

Mr Pangborn: *Oh no, Gloria Jean . . . not like that. Like this!*

He squeaks a cadenza like a deaf lark. The Foreman comes on.

Foreman: *Lunch. One hour.*

Some workmen go off, others come on with lunch boxes. There is general excitement and hurry.

Workmen pass the enthusiastic Mr Pangborn.

Mr Pangborn: *Now, Gloria Jean, you've got to do this number all the way through.*

The Pianist on his stool starts to play.

Gloria looks off wearily.

On the stage, the script girl sits beside the standing Mr

24

Pangborn and Gloria, who begins to sing cadenzas as the Pianist plays. Johnson comes on with a chair and just manages to place it under Mr Pangborn as he sits down. Mr Pangborn listens raptly.

Johnson dozes in a seat by the camera.

Gloria sings on with the Pianist playing and Mr Pangborn and the script girl listening. Superimposed over this scene, we see a montage of:

A time clock, with the hands pointing to 11:47. It moves up as a man's hands punch out his time-card.

Men's hands opening lunch boxes.

A man drinking from a paper cup.

A man with a watermelon.

The time-clock, now registering 12:47. It moves up again as men's hands punch in their time-cards.

The montage scenes fade, so that we are now back in the original scene of Gloria Jean singing to Mr Pangborn. Only now the workmen are coming back from their lunch, taking up their tools again.

Gloria: *We'll laugh and play/For 'tis Springtime . . .*

As she trills her cadenzas, the music stops, and we see that the Pianist is asleep on his stool.

As the workmen move about, making a noise behind Mr Pangborn, we track with Gloria as she goes over to wake the sleeping Pianist and turns the pages of music for him, so that they can finish the last few cadenzas together. Once done, she slumps down, her bored mouth staying open for a yawn.

Mr Pangborn makes a sign of command.

Johnson suddenly wakes up by the camera, and blows his whistle.

The Foreman, grinning with delight, yells.

Foreman: *Timber!*

A huge wood flat thuds to the stage an inch away from Mr Pangborn. Terrified, he leaps into an elevator nearby, which immediately begins rising into the air.

Mr Pangborn: *Stop it! Stop it!*

Now we dissolve to the outside of the studio, where Gloria

25

is standing at the gate talking to a cop. Extras hang about as FIELDS himself comes on. GLORIA runs over to him.

GLORIA : *Oh, hello, Uncle Bill.*

They hug each other and break like teddy bears.

GLORIA : *Where are you going?*

W. C. FIELDS : *I'm going in to the studio to read my script.*

GLORIA : *Don't you think I'd better go in with you?*

W. C. FIELDS : *Oh no, dear, I'll be all right.*

GLORIA : *Don't let them chisel you.*

By some bushes, BUTCH and BUDDY rise and look over to where an OLD LADY is sitting on a bench. We move nearby with the two boys.

W. C. FIELDS off : *I won't dear. You ought to be in there rehearsing with . . .*

FIELDS and GLORIA still stand in the driveway.

W. C. FIELDS : *. . . Buddy and Butch.*

GLORIA : *I can't find them.*

W. C. FIELDS : *Well, go in . . .*

By the bushes, the OLD LADY watches as BUTCH and BUDDY come out and BUDDY tosses a brick.

W. C. FIELDS off : *. . . there and look for 'em.*

As FIELDS is about to plant a kiss on GLORIA's forehead, the brick hits him on the back of the head.

W. C. FIELDS : *Godfrey Daniels!*

His hat falls off.

By the bushes, the two boys duck under cover and the OLD LADY hides herself behind her newspaper.

On the driveway, FIELDS rubs his head, while GLORIA picks up the brick and starts to throw it. Her uncle stops her.

W. C. FIELDS : *Uh-uh-uh-uh-uh! Hold your temper. Count ten!*

GLORIA suppresses her rage. The poised brick is slowly let down, while her lips count to ten.

But FIELDS stops GLORIA from actually dropping the brick.

W. C. FIELDS : *Now let 'er go. You got a good aim!*

GLORIA aims.

Back at the bushes, the OLD LADY peeks round her paper, as BUTCH and BUDDY crawl through the bushes. The brick sails on and hits the hidden BUDDY, who springs up, rubbing his head.

Back on the drive, FIELDS watches his niece with admiration, as she rushes off.

W. C. FIELDS : *That's a beauty!*

By the bushes, the two boys run away, yelling, as the screaming GLORIA runs on, chasing them. The OLD LADY watches happily.

Dissolve to a glass door.

On the door is printed the name of MR PANGBORN. The shadow of W. C. FIELDS falls on the glass

Inside the reception room, a SECRETARY is seated at her desk near a switchboard. FIELDS comes in to speak to her.

W. C. FIELDS : *Ah, good morning. I have an engagement for a story conference.*

The SECRETARY is facing the switchboard and she speaks nastily into the receiver, as if to FIELDS.

SECRETARY : *You big hoddy-doddy!*

FIELDS looks about himself, confused. There is nobody else there.

SECRETARY off : *You smoke cigars all day, and drink whiskey half . . .*

Now we see the girl at the switchboard speaking, while FIELDS sits down, throws his cigar into the ash can, and puts his hand guiltily into his pocket.

SECRETARY : *. . . the night.*

FIELDS now takes two more cigars from his pocket and throws them away.

SECRETARY off : *Someday you'll drown in a vat of whiskey!*

FIELDS talks to his hat.

W. C. FIELDS : *Drown in a vat of whiskey! Death, where is thy sting!*

The SECRETARY finishes her conversation into the receiver.

SECRETARY : *Good-bye!*

She turns off the telephone with a click.

FIELDS rises, feeling he had better get out before things get worse.

W. C. FIELDS : *Thank you, darling. Shortest interview on record.*

As he starts to leave, she stops him.

SECRETARY : *I beg your pardon. What did you say?*

27

FIELDS draws himself up to his full height.

W. C. FIELDS: *I have an engagement to read my script.*

The SECRETARY will not let him get by so easily.

SECRETARY: *What was the name?*

Now MR PANGBORN comes in, as FIELDS stands by the desk.

W. C. FIELDS: *Ahh . . . W. C. . . . Bill Fields.*

PANGBORN: *Oh, glad to know you, Mr Fields.*

W. C. FIELDS: *Glad to know you, Pangborn.*

MR PANGBORN: *Step right into my office.*

W. C. FIELDS: *Thank you . . . I will too.*

Pan with them as they start to go into the private office. FIELDS steps into a waste-basket. There is laughter and chat.

MR PANGBORN: *I'm sorry.*

As the two men go into the other office, we dissolve to its interior, where they now stand, laughing. FIELDS picks up a golf club and takes a swing at some golf balls lying on the carpet. He hits one which bounces round the room and hits him on the head.

W. C. FIELDS: *Well, watch your step here. Oh, drat! Ohhh, drat!*

MR PANGBORN: *You all right, Fields?*

FIELDS now kicks the golf balls into a portable golf-hole, and a bell rings, as MR PANGBORN looks down in amazement.

Into the room comes MRS HEATHER PANGBORN. She hits FIELDS with the door on the way to kiss her husband.

MR PANGBORN: *Hello, dear. Ahhh. Pardon me, Mr Fields, but my wife is not going to be dragged in and out of your picture by the hair of her head.*

W. C. FIELDS: *Of course, this is only a rough draft. You've got to bear with me half a tick. And . . .*

As MRS PANGBORN looks off haughtily, FIELDS' hand comes on and fingers her veil.

W. C. FIELDS off: *. . . You'll have to take that crab net off, dear. Here's one of the scenes.*

Now we see FIELDS holding the script, as MR and MRS PANGBORN pass him on their way to the desk.

W. C. FIELDS: *Do you mind being seated?*

MR PANGBORN: *Oh no . . . no.*

We pan with FIELDS as he joins the PANGBORNS, reading his script.

28

W. C. FIELDS: *Ah, you pass the pool hall . . . They're playing for the championship of the world . . . including . . .*
    MRS HEATHER PANGBORN looks off, utterly bored, seated on the desk.

W. C. FIELDS off: *. . . the two-dollar side bet . . .*
    MR PANGBORN is also seated and looks off warily.

W. C. FIELDS off: *You're riding in a jeep . . .*
    FIELDS is again seen by the PANGBORNS, reading his script. He ends by sitting down beside them.

W. C. FIELDS: *. . . on the sidewalk with a sailor . . . The scene intrigues you. You hop off while it's going . . .*
    FIELDS enjoys the script he is reading.

W. C. FIELDS: *. . . Then in the circus scene you wear a beard.*
    MRS HEATHER PANGBORN is furious.

MRS PANGBORN: *I wear a beard?*
    FIELDS acts out the beard.

W. C. FIELDS: *Yeah, a small beard . . . A Van Dyke . . . Just a little . . . You know what a Van Dyke is, don't you?*
    PANGBORN'S wife is disgusted.

MRS PANGBORN: *I certainly do.*
    FIELDS looks back at his script.

W. C. FIELDS: *Oh . . . er . . .*
    As FIELDS reads on to his uneasy audience, the scrubwoman MRS PASTROME comes in with her broom and bucket and cleaning stuff. She sets everything down, then crosses to the desk with the broom.

W. C. FIELDS: *You enter the pool hall . . . The contender for the championship just ripped the cloth which causes the ball . . .*

MRS PASTROME: *Good morning, Mr Pangborn.*

MR PANGBORN: *Good morning, Mrs Pastrome.*
    As FIELDS goes on reading his script at the desk, MRS PASTROME knocks him with her broom, which looks like a large droopy moustache.

W. C. FIELDS: *Take that Groucho Marx out of here, please.*
    MRS PASTROME does her job round the three seated at the desk. FIELDS reads on from his script.

W. C. FIELDS: *. . . which causes the ball to leap off the table . . .*
    MRS PASTROME starts to throw away FIELDS' hat. He grabs it.

W. C. FIELDS: *Just a moment, please.*

The telephone rings. MR PANGBORN picks up a telephone. No answer. He picks up a second telephone.

MR PANGBORN : *Hello. Oh, hello . . . yes, yes, she's here.*

MRS PASTROME has picked up her cleaning stuff to go out, but she dumps it as MR PANGBORN hands her the telephone.

MR PANGBORN : *It's for you, Mrs Pastrome.*

MRS PASTROME : *Uh.*

She leans across MR PANGBORN as she yells down the receiver and FIELDS tries to go on with his script.

W. C. FIELDS : *Strong men faint . . . some feints with their right . . . some feints with their left.*

MRS PASTROME : *Hello . . . yes . . . I can't hear you You'll have to talk louder. I'm talking as loud as I can. Don't we always have spaghetti for dinner? All right, we'll have raviolis . . . Of course, I'll go home. What time is it? Yes . . . I can't hear you. Good-bye.*

W. C. FIELDS : *He feints . . . yeah . . . yeah . . . and you rush over and put his head in your lap. Now good-bye.*

MRS PASTROME dumps the receiver on the desk and moves off. MR PANGBORN picks up the receiver and hangs it back on the telephone.

MR PANGBORN : *Thank you, Mrs Pastrome.*

MRS PASTROME turns round by the door.

MRS PASTROME : *You're welcome.*

MR PANGBORN winces as the door slams on her. At the desk, FIELDS ploughs on through the script and plays it out.

W. C. FIELDS : *Then you go off to the local barber shop and get shaved and play the rest of the scene and the picture with an absolutely clean face.*

MRS HEATHER PANGBORN squirms.

MR PANGBORN looks off, squints and rubs his hands together. FIELDS looks from one to the other at the desk.

W. C. FIELDS : *Oh . . . well, all right . . . we can cut that out.*

At the desk, MR PANGBORN smiles benignly, reaches across and gets the script.

MR PANGBORN : *If you don't mind, Mr Fields, I'll read it myself. I get a better feel . . . er . . . capture the mood and tempo better that way. It's in English, isn't it?* Clears his throat and starts to read. *Long Shot of streamlined plane with open air observation compart . . . an open air rear observation compartment! In the plane is the handsome hero, Bill Fields* . . .

Mrs Heather Pangborn can't believe her ears.

Mr Pangborn goes on with the script.

Mr Pangborn: . . . *and his little niece, Gloria Jean, who are winging their way towards the Russian willage* . . .

Dissolve to a long shot of an aeroplane flying above the clouds at night. Over the noise of the engines, Mr Pangborn reads on.

Mr Pangborn off: . . . *in the strange and distant land of* . . .

As Mr Pangborn's voice dies away, we dissolve to the interior of a large compartment on an aeroplane. Fields and Gloria Jean sit facing each other, while a stewardess and a large Turk go on and off.

W. C. Fields: *Are you happy?*

Gloria: *You bet I am, Uncle.*

Fields looks suspiciously at the Turk.

W. C. Fields: *Must be a Shriner's Convention in town.*

Gloria looks off and laughs.

Fields still considers the odds.

W. C. Fields: *Or maybe he's a cigarette salesman.*

Now an Englishman, loaded with sports gear for tennis and golf and croquet, passes Fields and his niece.

Englishman: *I beg your pardon.*

Fields dodges the golf clubs as the Englishman goes off to play.

W. C. Fields: *It doesn't matter. I hope he hasn't brought his polo ponies on board with him. They'll be pawing all night and keep us awake.*

Gloria smiles at the joke.

Again we see the plane flying above the night clouds. Then we dissolve to the corridor of the plane, where Gloria is standing in her pyjamas with her uncle. He kisses her.

Gloria: *Good night, Uncle.*

W. C. Fields: *Good night, dear. Now don't you worry. I'll be right over there in the upper berth next to you.*

Gloria: *All right.*

She gets into the lower berth, then we see her inside the drawn curtains as she settles herself down.

In the corridor of the plane, FIELDS stands watching the
ENGLISHMAN coming on and bending down to rub his ankle.

W. C. FIELDS: *What's the matter? Did you sprain your ankle?*

ENGLISHMAN: *Er ... no ... no ... no ... a dog ... er ... bit me.*

W. C. FIELDS: *Oh.*

ENGLISHMAN: *I was playing ... er, croquet ... and ... er
... I dropped my mallet and er ... a little Daschund ran straight
out and er ... and er ... grabbed me by the fetlock.*

W. C. FIELDS: *Oh, rather fortunate that it wasn't a Newfound-
land dog that bit you.*

ENGLISHMAN: *Yes, yes ... rather ... I suppose so ... yes
... I'm sleeping here somewhere but I don't know where.*

W. C. FIELDS: *Oh well, there's no other place to sleep if you don't
sleep in the plane here.*

ENGLISHMAN: *That's right.*

W. C. FIELDS: *No, no hotels around anywhere.*

The ENGLISHMAN totters away.

Inside his berth, the huge TURK unwraps his cummerbund.
As FIELDS stands in the corridor, the STEWARDESS comes in
with the steps for the upper berths, which she puts into place.

STEWARDESS: *Here you are, Mr Fields.*

W. C. FIELDS: *Oh, thank you. Eh, where are you supposed to
sleep? In that little hammock up there?*

STEWARDESS: *Yes, sir.*

Just as Uncle Bill is working something out and mounting the
steps, GLORIA opens the curtains of her berth and sticks her
head out.

GLORIA: *Good-night, Uncle Bill.*

W. C. FIELDS off: *Good-night, dear.*

He looks inside his berth and flicks at a fly and looks down.

W. C. FIELDS: *I'll be right across the way, dear. I'll be up here
all alone ... except for that fly. Get out of here!*

In the corridor, the STEWARDESS helps FIELDS to crawl into
the upper berth, pushing at his bulk.

W. C. FIELDS off: *Get the other leg, please. Thanks.*

Inside his berth, he lies down.

W. C. FIELDS: *I use both of them ... There's some answers in my
hat ...*

Muttering, he puts his hat over his face.

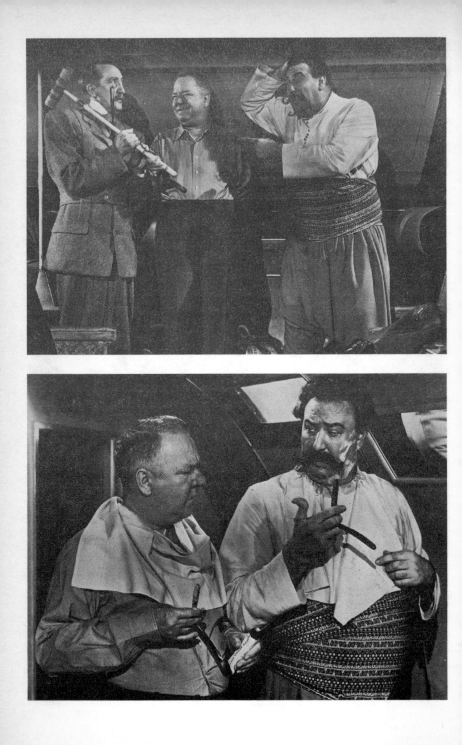

Inside another berth, the huge TURK is still unwrapping his cummerbund.

Dissolve to a shot of the plane flying above the clouds, this time in the sunshine.

Along the corridor, the STEWARDESS comes up to FIELDS' berth.

STEWARDESS: *Time to get up, sir. We're landing shortly.*

Inside his berth, the TURK begins wrapping up his cummerbund. In the struggle, he hits his feet on the end of the berth, and yells with agony.

With a cry of pain, FIELDS leans partly out of his berth, rubbing his head.

STEWARDESS: *Are you air-sick?*

W. C. FIELDS: *No, dear, somebody put too many olives in my martinis last night.*

STEWARDESS: *Could I get you a bromo?*

W. C. FIELDS: *No, I couldn't stand the noise.*

Below the peering FIELDS, the STEWARDESS bends down to GLORIA's lower berth.

STEWARDESS: *Time to get up . . .*

Inside her berth, GLORIA wakes.

STEWARDESS off: *. . . little lady.*

W. C. FIELDS off: *Get up, dear.*

GLORIA: *O.K.*

As the STEWARDESS walks off, FIELDS leans further out of his berth to talk to GLORIA.

W. C. FIELDS: *We are landing in a few minutes . . . er one-half hour. Two or three or what time did she say we are landing? Maybe we're not going to land. Go back to sleep again.*

He sinks back behind the curtains of his berth and begins to sing.

W. C. FIELDS: *Chickens . . .*

In her berth, GLORIA smiles to hear her uncle sing.

W. C. FIELDS off: *. . . they lay eggs in Kansas/Chickens they lay eggs in Kansas/Chickens lay eggs as big as nutmegs/The chickens lay eggs in Kansas.*

A BLONDE also lies in her berth, amused by the song.

W. C. FIELDS off: *The chickens have pretty legs in Kansas . . .*

The STEWARDESS smiles to hear the song.

W. C. Fields off: *Chickens have pretty legs in Kansas* . . .
The Blonde is still amused.
W. C. Fields off: *It's really not a joke/One rolled me for my poke*
. . .
The Stewardess is also happy.
W. C. Fields off: *Chickens have pretty legs in Kansas.*
The plane flies on above the sunny clouds.
Dissolve to Fields and the Englishman sitting by the windows of the plane.
W. C. Fields: *Ah, those clouds look just as fleecy as* . . . *clouds.*
The Turk comes on, arranging his flowing dress and feeling his baggy trousers. Fields feels them too.
W. C. Fields: *Hm* . . . *enough material there for a Ringling Brothers* . . .
The glaring Turk turns round.
W. C. Fields off: . . . *big top. Maybe a smuggler.*
The Turk glares above Fields and the Englishman.
Turk: *You a big nose have it!*
W. C. Fields: *Oh, that's a surprise to me.*
Englishman: *I say, I should take that as a personal insult.*
W. C. Fields: *Yeah, I should too.*
Turk to the Englishman: *I you hate too.*
W. C. Fields: *He hates you too.*
The Turk parts the curtains of a lower berth and crawls in, leaving only his feet showing.
Fields now rises, muttering. In his hand is the Englishman's croquet mallet. The Englishman half-heartedly tries to stop the massacre of Islam.
Englishman: Here, here, I say. Half a tick, old man, half a tick.
By the lower berth, Fields creeps up with the mallet. The head of the Turk is outlined against the curtains. Fields hits the Turk's head with the mallet and gets out. The Turk opens the curtains and rubs his head, yelling.
Back by the seats, the Englishman tries to wrest the mallet from the victorious Fields.
Englishman: *Steady on, old man. Steady on.*
The sitting Turk rises in wrath from his berth and seeks revenge, puffing and blowing.
As the Turk charges on, Fields lets the Englishman seize

the mallet back from him.

W. C. FIELDS: *I have a big nose, have I . . . eh?*

TURK to the ENGLISHMAN: *You! Me on the head hitted!*

The snorting TURK grabs the ENGLISHMAN by the neck in a terrible hold.

W. C. FIELDS: *Say, boys, let me out of this thing. I am neutral. Go ahead.*

The TURK hauls the ENGLISHMAN off and throws him back across the compartment, while FIELDS stands aside.

Dissolve to the washroom, where FIELDS comes on carrying his shaving brush and tooth brush. The TURK comes in, puts his shaving kit nearby, and crosses over to wash at the basin, as FIELDS tries to squeeze out.

W. C. FIELDS: *Ah, forgot my soap, forgot my razor, forgot everything.*

TURK: *Pardon me.*

The TURK pushes the protesting FIELDS aside as he washes his hands and admires his terrible face in the mirror.

W. C. FIELDS: *No wonder they call this a giant airliner. Do you travel as one person, or do you get a party rate of ten?*

FIELDS begins juggling around the toilet articles with the TURK joining in the act. He tries to steal the TURK's toothpaste.

W. C. FIELDS: *O.K. Don't laugh, then. Oh, here you are . . .*

TURK: *Thank you.*

W. C. FIELDS: *You are welcome.*

TURK: *I didn't sleep well last night.*

W. C. FIELDS: *You didn't, eh?*

TURK: *I am troubled with insomnia.*

W. C. FIELDS: *Oh, insomnia? Oh well, I know a good cure for it.*

TURK: *Yeah?*

W. C. FIELDS: *Get plenty of sleep.*

TURK: *Sleep?* He laughs.

W. C. FIELDS: *That's what the doctor told me. I hope he isn't on the plane in the morning when I get off.*

Now the TURK brushes his teeth as if he were scrubbing infidels clean. FIELDS tries to teach him dental hygiene, while putting the rest of the TURK's toiletries in his pocket.

W. C. FIELDS: *Excuse me. Always brush 'em down like that. Never across like that.*

The TURK froths and mutters.

W. C. FIELDS: *That's what it says in the latest etiquette book. Yeah. I don't need any more.*

Dissolve to another shot of the washroom, with FIELDS jumping up behind the TURK to try and shave, but the TURK completely blocks the view. So FIELDS has to scrape away as best he can.

Dissolve to the plane, now flying through the clouds.

Now the TURK and FIELDS have their backs to us, and both are shaving with their faces reflected in the mirror, their hands scraping away.

Now we fade into a close-up which shows them shaving each other with the fierce sound of snapping bristles.

W. C. FIELDS: *Ha ha! Must have just gone through a cloud. Huh . . . that's a hot one! You're shaving me and I'm shaving you!*

TURK: *Uh.*

The plane flies on above the clouds.

Dissolve to GLORIA, now seated and primping herself.

FIELDS comes to join her.

W. C. FIELDS: *Are you ready, dear?*

GLORIA: *Be ready in a jiffy.*

W. C. FIELDS: *Ah . . . a jiffy. Oh . . . O.K. Well, I'll meet you on the back platform, dear*

GLORIA: *All right.*

W. C. FIELDS: *O.K.*

In the compartment, two LADIES are seated with a MAN. The stewardess comes on and steps aside for FIELDS, who accosts her.

W. C. FIELDS: *Hello, dear.*

A LADY: *Oh, miss.*

Losing his quarry to her job, FIELDS marches on.

The rear platform of the giant airliner is, indeed, open to the clouds, as on the back of an old continental train. FIELDS comes over, and we pan with him as he sits. He takes a glass of water from the table and throws it overboard. The slipstream of the airliner throws it right back in his face.

W. C. FIELDS: *What inclement weather!*

He takes a whisky bottle from his pocket and pours himself a drink, then he stands the bottle on the window-ledge of the platform. GLORIA comes up behind him.

GLORIA: *What are you drinking, Uncle Bill?*

W. C. FIELDS: *Oh, just a little ginger ale, dear. Pull up a chair.*
GLORIA pulls up a chair and sits beside her uncle.

GLORIA earnestly: *You know, Uncle Bill, I've been thinking. Why didn't you ever marry?*

FIELDS considers this unpleasing prospect before answering her.

W. C. FIELDS: *I was in love with a beautiful blonde once, dear. She drove me to drink. That's the one thing I'm indebted to her for.*
GLORIA laughs and laughs.

FIELDS now wants another drink, so he is full of good advice.

W. C. FIELDS: *Go in and push your little portmanteau, will you, dear?*

GLORIA: *All right.*

Track back as she rises and leaves the rear platform. As she goes, FIELDS starts to reach for his whiskey bottle. He is not looking properly and knocks the bottle off the window ledge. He rises, appalled. Quickly, he dives over the edge of the aeroplane. GLORIA runs back to the window.

GLORIA: *Uncle Bill!*

A trick shot shows us FIELDS falling through the clouds, clutching his hat.

The wind blows at GLORIA's hair, as she yells at the window.

GLORIA: *Uncle Bill!*

Another trick shot shows FIELDS still falling through the clouds. He catches up with the whiskey bottle, grabs it, pulls the cork out of the air, and caps the bottle.

From high above, we see a large house surrounded by gardens in the mountains.

Now we are in the gardens, as the beautiful young OULIOTTA HEMOGLOBEN goes over to the divan and lies upon it. Close now on OULIOTTA, as we see her looking up from the pillows and rising in surprise, as a human bomb hurtles down. Another trick shot shows FIELDS still falling through the clouds, as he poises his hands, ready to dive.

OULIOTTA runs from the divan and crosses the terrace to the steps. Shot from directly overhead we see FIELDS falling onto

45

the divan with the sound of thunder, then bouncing up again, while OULIOTTA watches him from the terrace.

OULIOTTA is bewildered, but beautifully so. FIELDS is still bouncing up and down on the divan. Finally, he reaches equipoise, or somewhat near.

OULIOTTA goes on watching him, unable to believe her eyes. FIELDS slowly gets to his feet, as OULIOTTA comes on. He doesn't notice her at first, then does a double take when he does.

W. C. FIELDS : *Whew! Ah, why didn't I think of that parachute? Well, there she goes! Whew, what a bump! And how unfortunate . . . ah, ah, how do you do?*

He approaches the amazed OULIOTTA.

W. C. FIELDS : *Uh . . . you live here?*

OULIOTTA : *What are you?*

W. C. FIELDS : *I am an American citizen.*

OULIOTTA : *An American eagle?*

W. C. FIELDS : *Why, no, first time I have ever been up in a plane in my life. I'm . . . uh . . . just a man.*

OULIOTTA : *Man? I have never heard that word before.*

W. C. FIELDS : *You didn't?*

OULIOTTA : *Are you really a man?*

W. C. FIELDS : *Well, I have been called other things.*

Perplexed, the lovely OULIOTTA eyes her first man.

OULIOTTA : *I have never seen one before in all my life.*

FIELDS relishes the dialogue, seeing nobody else near.

W. C. FIELDS : *You never have . . . eh?*

OULIOTTA : *Mother brought me to the nest here when I was only three months old.*

W. C. FIELDS : *Oh, she did, eh? You have never seen a man? Have you ever played the game of Squidgilum?*

OULIOTTA shakes her head in sorrow.

OULIOTTA : *No, the only game I have ever played is bean bag.*

FIELDS sees his chance, and gets a chair.

W. C. FIELDS : *Bean bag? Hm . . . that's very good. It becomes very exciting at times. I saw the championship played in Paris. Many people were killed. Pull up a chair*

Obediently, OULIOTTA pulls up a chair close to his chair and sits down.

W. C. FIELDS : *Get a little closer. Wait a minute, maybe I'm the one.*

He puts his hands over his head as he starts to explain the game.

W. C. FIELDS : *Uh, now you put your hands on your head that way.*

Now she puts her hands over her head and follows his game plan.

W. C. FIELDS : *That's it. Now close your eyes and pucker your lips a bit.*

He leans over and kisses her.

OULIOTTA is now seen in a large close-up. FIELDS, with his back to us, withdraws. She opens her eyes and lowers her arms, then decides that she likes the game.

So she puts her arms over her head again, closes her eyes and puckers up her mouth.

FIELDS does another double take to see OULIOTTA ready, willing and able again. So he gives her a second kiss. Then she lowers her arms.

From the house, OULIOTTA's black-clad ogre of a mother, MRS. HEMOGLOBEN, appears, holding a Great Dane with vampire fangs on a leash.

The Great Dane looks gigantic, seen in close-up and movement.

Now the Great Lover is seen in close-up and delighted.

W. C. FIELDS : *Ah ... shall we play another rubber?*

OULIOTTA smiles, then hears the Great Dane growl, and she looks off.

OULIOTTA : *Why, Mother!*

FIELDS now looks round, scared at the canine and maternal menace.

The Great Dane's head slavers at him.

MRS HEMOGLOBEN's face glares at him.

FIELDS decides to brave it out beside OULIOTTA.

W. C. FIELDS : *Romulus and Remus!*

MRS HEMOGLOBEN glares back.

MRS HEMOGLOBEN : *What are you doing here?*

She joins her daughter and FIELDS.

OULIOTTA : *Mother, this is a man. He fell out of an aeroplane and*

47

brought a wonderful new game to us.

MRS HEMOGLOBEN glares even more ferociously.

OULIOTTA off : *It is called Squidgilum.*

OULIOTTA demonstrates the game beside the uneasy FIELDS.

OULIOTTA : *You pull two chairs together, place your hands on your head in this fashion, then you close your eyes, then you both press your lips together.*

MRS HEMOGLOBEN is suddenly transformed with delight. She smiles and raises her arms.

MRS HEMOGLOBEN : *I'll try it with him. Mother knows best.*

OULIOTTA poses, then closes her eyes.

OULIOTTA : *Close your eyes, Mother.*

As MRS HEMOGLOBEN waits with eyes closed, FIELDS approaches, sees what is in store, picks up his hat, and hurries off. While OULIOTTA and her mother still wait with lowered lids, their arms over their heads and lips puckered, FIELDS runs hurriedly over to the steps and starts through an arch. The other side of the arch, there is a basket on a crank and a windlass set in front of mountains. FIELDS dives into the basket, which plunges downwards on its rope.

Back near the divan in the garden MRS HEMOGLOBEN and OULIOTTA stand waiting. They drop their arms, open their eyes. Pan with them as they start towards the steps.

As the basket falls down the cliff face, FIELDS rises out of it and looks about him.

By the archway, mother and daughter try to catch the crank as the rope unwinds.

FIELDS still plunges down the cliff-face in the basket, but he manages to find two cigarettes in his pocket.

At the railing by the cliff's edge, MRS HEMOGLOBEN gives OULIOTTA a homily.

MRS HEMOGLOBEN : *Men! Men! They are all alike. They'll deceive you as your father did me. He kissed a chorus girl and when I found it out, he said : 'Oh, I was drunk and didn't know what I was doing.'*

OULIOTTA : *Do you think he drinks?*

MRS HEMOGLOBEN : *He didn't get that nose from playing ping-pong.*

The basket hits a platform at the base of the cliff. FIELDS is jolted out onto the road below. There is the sound of breaking glass.

FIELDS sits up on the road and takes his broken whiskey-bottle out of his pocket and regards it.

W. C. FIELDS : *What a catastrophe!*

Dissolve to a close-up of MR PANGBORN in his office, still seated at his desk. He slams the script onto the desk top. Pan with him as he rises.

MR PANGBORN scathing : *Just a minute, Mr Fields! There's a limit to everything. This script is an insult to a man's intelligence. Even mine!*

FIELDS listens, seated on the desk.

MR PANGBORN off : *You drop from a plane ten thousand feet in the air . . .*

MRS HEATHER PANGBORN also listens, chin in hand.

MR PANGBORN off : *And you land on a divan without a scratch . . .*

MR PANGBORN is emphatic and gesturing. Pan with him as he sinks back into his chair.

MR PANGBORN : *You play post-office with a beautiful blonde and then you throw yourself over a cliff in a basket! It's impossible! Inconceivable! Incomprehensible! And besides that . . . it's no good!*

FIELDS sits on the desk, looking at him.

MR PANGBORN continues his harangue.

MR PANGBORN : *And as for the continuity . . . it's . . . it's terrible! And for my own information . . . off the record . . . what's happened to Gloria Jean? Where's she been all this time?*

He picks up the script, finds the place, starts to read it.

MR PANGBORN : *Oh, I . . . Oh, I see . . . Here she is . . . Poor little Gloria, almost in tears waiting at . . .*

Dissolve to GLORIA JEAN seated on a bench outside an airport. A HOSTESS is talking on the telephone in a nearby booth. She comes out to GLORIA.

MR PANGBORN off : *. . . the airport, not knowing which way to turn, when suddenly . . .*

HOSTESS : *Telephone, honey.*

GLORIA gets up and runs to the booth.

Once inside it, she answers the phone, rather surprised.

GLORIA : *Hello. Uncle Bill! Where are you? What? Yes! Yes, I'll be right over!*

She hangs up the receiver, leaves the booth.

She goes back to the HOSTESS and both go off from the airport.

GLORIA : *How . . . How do I get to the Russian Village?*

HOSTESS : *I'll take care of you.*

Dissolve to a long shot of a Russian Village, very studio style, with folksy peasants wandering about and wondering what they are doing there in those clothes. Dissolve to the end of a cantina bar, where FIELDS has struck liquor again in the desert. He is now wearing an astrakhan hat and recounting his adventures to two new cronies, ROBERTS and PETER CARSON, a handsome young engineer.

W. C. FIELDS : *I fell out of an aeroplane whilst trying to retrieve a bottle of golden nectar . . .*

Outside the cantina, LEON ERROL is passing in his Mexican sombrero. He steps inside to listen to the tale.

W. C. FIELDS off : *And landed on the pinnacle of yonder rock . . .*

FIELDS continues weaving his words to his bar buddies.

W. C. FIELDS : *Where is domiciled a vision of loveliness if ever there was one. And her mother . . . a buzzard . . . if ever there was one!*

ERROL stands by the door, still listening.

CARSON off : *If that girl is as beautiful as you say . . .*

CARSON and ROBERTS lean on the bar, fascinated.

CARSON : *I'll scale the wall tomorrow.*

ROBERTS now joins in to give FIELDS the low-down.

ROBERTS : *I've heard about them. They say the old buzzard's husband walked out on 'em before the girl was born. And the buzzard vowed that the daughter would never see nor hear the name 'man' as long as she lived. They also say the old girl has a bank-roll so big a greyhound couldn't leap over it.*

FIELDS is now seen in calculating close-up, his eyes narrowing under his fez.

W. C. FIELDS : *Yeah?*

The noise of a Russian chorus sounds off, as ERROL listens by the cantina doorway.

W. C. FIELDS : *Well, she seems to have a kind heart, too.*

By the doorway, ERROL rubs his hands, smiling. The Russian chorus sounds louder.

W. C. FIELDS off : *May be you could . . .*

FIELDS talks on, plotting gently.

W. C. FIELDS : *. . . induce her to come down, and talk turkey, to one that really loves her and has her interest at heart. She seemed like an awfully nice woman to me . . . now that I come to think of it.*

The music has reached a crescendo, as we cut to a long shot of a country road, where GLORIA and a FARMER now ride with a Russian-type cart through some trees. Pan with them as the cart pulls up.

RUSSIAN CHORUS : **Kak loob loo ya vas · · ·**

The singing peasants squat or stand, some of them playing rural instruments. GLORIA and the FARMER ride towards them.

RUSSIAN CHORUS : **Kak boyoos ya vas . . .**

In various shots, GLORIA is seen to join in the ancient foreign ditty from the top of the cart, both still and moving.

RUSSIAN CHORUS :   **Znat u vi diel vas**
                     Ya v'nie do bry tchas . . .

GLORIA :   **Otchi tchnorniya**
                     Otchi strassniya
                     Otchi zhgootchiya
                     Yi pre krassniya . . . [1]

She then repeats the words of the chorus.

Back in the cantina, we can see men drinking at the tables and FIELDS with CARSON and ROBERTS at the bar, as GLORIA's voice trills with the Russian chorus. FIELDS obviously knows who the little nightingale is.

---

[1] This time the titles under the folksy bits read :

CHORUS : *Since our looks have crossed*
          No more peace I've known
          But the world's well lost
          For your eyes alone
GLORIA : *Eyes as black as night*
          Eyes so starry bright
          Eyes that penetrate
          Like the glance of Fate.

51

Now we go back to the FARMER and GLORIA singing in the moving cart with the peasants following her. She finishes in a Niagara of cadenzas.

Fade into the cantina bar again, where the BARTENDER is now watching FIELDS in a huddle with his rival, LEON ERROL.

ERROL : *Hey, hey, two goat's milk.*

Hands place two glasses and a bottle before FIELDS and ERROL standing at the bar.

W. C. FIELDS : *Two what?*

ERROL : *Uh-huh . . . you'll love it.*

ERROL pours the drinks from a bottle full of white fluid.

W. C. FIELDS : *Not so sure about that.*

ERROL : *Yeah, yeah, . . . it's a great drink.*

W. C. FIELDS : *Haven't you any Red-Eye?*

ERROL drinking and gasping : *It's good! Good!*

He makes a face and puts a cigarette in his mouth, which he lights in a candle. FIELDS looks at his goat's milk as if it was a grenade.

FIELDS : *Well, it hasn't killed you.*

ERROL : *Of course not.*

Very dubiously, FIELDS drains his glass of goats' milk. He blows against the candle. A large flame flares out of it once, twice.

Back on the waggon, GLORIA waves to the following peasants from beside the DRIVER.

At the entrance to the cantina, FIELDS comes forward, followed by CARSON and a MAN.

The waggon pulls up, and GLORIA smiles at the DRIVER and gets off in front of him, holding her bag.

GLORIA : *Uncle Bill!*

W. C. FIELDS off : *Hello, dear.*

DRIVER : **Das vidanya, Krasavitz.**

At the cantina entrance, GLORIA runs up to FIELDS to embrace him. A MAN takes her bag, while her uncle introduces her to CARSON and ROBERTS.

W. C. FELDS : *Dear, I'm so glad you arrived safely. Er . . . this is my er . . . little niece, Gloria Jean. This is Mister er . . .*

ROBERTS : *Roberts.*

W. C. Fields : *Mister Roberts and this is . . . er . . .*
Carson : *Carson.*
W. C. Fields : *Mister Carson. Yeah.*
   Gloria notices the drink in her uncle's hand.
Gloria : *What are you drinking, Uncle Bill?*
W. C. Fields : *I'm drinking goat's milk, dear.*
Gloria : *What kind of goat's milk?*
W. C. Fields : *Nanny goat's milk. It's very sweet.*

Dissolve to a long shot of a mountain peak with rugged scenery nearby, then dissolve again to the bottom of the cliff, where Carson is now on the platform. He stands on the steps and looks at the basket and the ropes above it. Then he runs at the ropes, tugs at them, jumps onto a rail and begins climbing the rocks behind.

On another part of the cliff, Leon Errol is scaling the rocks near the hanging ropes. He is dressed in full Alpine gear. He lassoes some rocks above, and works his way up the cliff. In a series of action shots, we see the lassoe rope catch the mountain peak, work loose and break, just as Errol leaps to safety on a ledge.

Elsewhere on the cliff, Carson climbs up.

On a high rock, Gargo the gorilla clings. Errol climbs up towards the gorilla, not seeing it.

With his back to the ape, Errol feels behind him on the rock, sits and looks downwards. He takes his pack off his back and a bottle of goat's milk from the pack, as the gorilla watches.

Errol starts to drink. Suddenly the gorilla grabs the bottle from him. Errol sees the ape and yells. He leaps up, facing the gorilla and falls.

Close on the gorilla, we see it looking down, holding the bottle. The ape puts its hands sadly to its eyes, then sniffs from the bottle, yells, and throws the bottle down after Errol before clambering away.

Carson is still scaling the cliff, not knowing what is above. The gorilla moves down the rocks on a rope to where Errol is lying unconscious in some bushes.

The gorilla's great hand lifts him up.

Then the gorilla carries him away up the face of the cliff.

53

CARSON has a hard time scaling the rocks. He tears at the bushes and the trees. He loses his balance, drops to a ledge and hangs on.

In the garden of the house, OULIOTTA'S mother, MRS HEMO-GLOBEN, goes over to the wall. The gorilla climbs up to her with ERROL over its shoulder. It throws ERROL down on the lawn and hops up and down on the wall.

MRS HEMOGLOBEN clapping her hands: *Gargo!* The gorilla snorts. *Gargo!* The gorilla roars. *Gargo!* On the wall, the gorilla yelps and raises his hands.

In the garden, MRS HEMOGLOBEN goes over to the lying ERROL and drags his body over to the door.

The Great Dane watches, slavering.

MRS HEMOGLOBEN drags ERROL inside the door and closes it. By the wall, OULIOTTA is looking down as the handsome CARSON pulls himself up below her. He looks at her and removes his hat.

CARSON: *Hello.*

OULIOTTA: *Hello.*

The gorilla poses on the wall.

CARSON climbs over the wall as OULIOTTA moves over to the steps. He comes up behind her, as she looks at him.

She smiles, then suddenly turns her head away shyly. Pan with her as she leaves the steps for a love seat, where she sits with CARSON.

Two monkeys chatter as they watch the scene.

OULIOTTA off: *Have you ever played Squidgilum?*

CARSON sits in the love seat as OULIOTTA goes through the motions of the game, arms up, eyes closed, mouth ready for a kiss.

CARSON: *No, I never heard of it.*

OULIOTTA: *Oh well, we . . . place our hands over our heads thus . . . then we close our eyes . . .then we press our lips together.*

CARSON is close now, staring at OULIOTTA.

One of the two monkeys puts its hands on its head as if to play Squidgilum, until the other one looks off.

The gorilla on the wall puts its hands on its head and smacks its lips.

54

OULIOTTA waits in the Squidgilum position. As nothing happens, she opens her eyes and closes them again.

OULIOTTA: *Go ahead.*

CARSON kisses her quickly. She smiles with pleasure.

OULIOTTA: *Hm . . . isn't it fun? The man that was up here yesterday said this was a national game where he came from.*

One of the two monkeys thumbs its nose, while the other gesticulates. OULIOTTA smiles, puts her hands on her head and purses her lips. CARSON leans forward and kisses her. Both of the two monkeys put their hands on their heads. The gorilla on the wall tactfully turns round.

OULIOTTA and CARSON embrace and kiss and smile.

OULIOTTA: *Hm . . . you must be a professional.*

CARSON: *Did the man who came up here yesterday play this game with you?*

OULIOTTA: *Yes, he did. But when Mother wanted to play . . . something frightened him and he dived over the parapet.*

CARSON: *Why, the old reprobate.*

Now we join the dazed ERROL and MRS HEMOGLOBEN, who are seated facing each other. She places his hands on his head and kisses him with the noise of a suction pump.

Back on OULIOTTA, as she smiles and raises her hands to her head.

OULIOTTA: *Let's play Squidgy!*

CARSON kisses her again and holds her close. The Great Dane comes along the garden path towards them.

It nods its huge head.

CARSON goes on kissing and holding OULIOTTA.

The Great Dane barks at CARSON.

CARSON barks back at the Great Dane.

The big dog runs off, scared, through the arch.

On top of a radio, one of the monkeys turns a dial to get some music.

CARSON looks around to see where the tune is coming from, as OULIOTTA rises and begins to sing.

OULIOTTA: *If a body meet a body*
   Comin' through the rye
   If a body kiss a body
   Need a body cry?

Every lassie has her laddie . . .

Track with OULIOTTA as she goes into a jive version of the old Scots ballad, dancing and jazzing it up. Her innocence is suddenly gone with the music, and she is a real hotcha babe.

OULIOTTA: *. . . None they say, hae I*
Yet, a' the lads they smile on me
Comin' through the rye . . .
When the body met the body
The body to the body said
Oh, body, you're somebody
You ought to get ahead.
Ev'ry lassie has her laddie
But I'll be dif'rent I think
I'm gonna find a daddy
To dress me up in mink
Then we'll ride, ride, ride
A-comin' through the rye, rye, rye
A-comin' through the rye
Yes indeed, daddy
We'll be comin' on through the rye . . .

Now we cut back to MR PANGBORN at his desk. He puts the script down, all burned up, and he shakes his finger.

MR PANGBORN: *Marvellous . . . wonderful . . . amazing! The girl has been living up a mountain-top since she was three months old . . . and for no reason at all . . . suddenly blossoms out with jumpin' jive! Do you actually think I'm a dope? Now don't you answer that.*

The seated FIELDS turns his head to mutter.

W. C. FIELDS: *Let's get on with it anyway.*

MR PANGBORN picks up the script and reads on.

We cut back to the garden, where OULIOTTA is now strolling over to CARSON with the camera moving with her. She sits beside him, her hands on her head again.

OULIOTTA: *Squidge!*

CARSON: *Are you sure you've lived here since you were three months old?*

The two young people kiss again.

The two monkeys again put their hands on their heads for Squidgilum. They squeal with delight.

Back to the seated ERROL and MRS HEMOGLOBEN.

ERROL: *Well ... who are you?*

MRS HEMOGLOBEN: *Mrs Hemogloben!*

ERROL: *Who?*

MRS HEMOGLOBEN: *Mrs Hemogloben!*

ERROL: *Give me another transfusion.* He kisses her. *Hemo ... Hemogloben ... oh, you're not the dame that has all the mo ... I mean the beautiful lady that has the house on top of the hill. Oh, all my life I've been craving love ... love ... yum-yum ...*

He grabs her and kisses her again. They both laugh with pleasure.

Down at the base of the cliff, W. C. FIELDS and GLORIA and BUTCH and BUDDY are now in the basket, with a mysterious RUSSIAN there to help with the bass fiddle. FIELDS wears a black frock coat and a seedy wedding outfit.

W. C. FIELDS: *I don't think you can get that cricket bat in here.*

RUSSIAN: *Yes ... sure.*

In the basket, GLORIA talks to FIELDS in front of the two boys.

GLORIA: *What kind of a bird is that, Uncle Bill?*

There is a small parrot on FIELDS' finger.

W. C. FIELDS off: *Oh, it's a Philillo bird, dear ...*

Back in the basket, FIELDS explains.

GLORIA: *Flies backwards?*

W. C. FIELDS: *Yes. It lives in the desert. Flies backwards to keep the sand out of its eyes.*

On the top of the mountain by the crank and the windlass, CARSON and OULIOTTA look down. He drops a little rock. All five are in the basket below, waiting. FIELDS looks around him for a switch or something.

W. C. FIELDS: *I wonder where the contraption is that starts this thing.*

The rock drops into FIELDS' hat on his head with a thud. He takes it off and looks up.

GLORIA: *Oh, did it hurt you, Uncle?*

W. C. FIELDS: *Now how could a rock dropping from a thousand feet hurt your head?*

CARSON and OULIOTTA look down from on high, and wave. The occupants of the basket look up and wave. CARSON and OULIOTTA turn the crank. The five in the basket begin to rise, as if under a balloon.

W. C. FIELDS: *Ah . . . here we go. You can see all over the country, can't you?*

CARSON and OULIOTTA turn the crank. The basket rises up the mountain. The two on the crank let it go. The rope whirls backwards, the basket drops down the face of the cliff, then suddenly stops.

CARSON is clutching the crank handle. OULIOTTA gets her grip again beside his hands.

In the basket close to the cliff face, FIELDS declares:

W. C. FIELDS: *Oh, it's for a Maxwell parachute!*

GLORIA: *What's a Maxwell parachute?*

W. C. FIELDS: *Good until the last drop, dear. Oh, here we go again.*

The basket rises. Now the basket nears the peak of the mountain. CARSON and OULIOTTA turn the crank. The basket rises to the top platform as the two lovers work at the windlass. MRS HEMOGLOBEN stops at the door of the house, looking off with her knitting bag in her hand. The two young lovers help FIELDS out of the basket. He has flowers in his hand, and the parrot on his finger.

W. C. FIELDS: *Ready, children . . .*

They process down through the archway, with BUTCH and BUDDY holding the tails of FIELDS' immense tail coat. A wedding march sounds from the bass fiddle. MRS HEMOGLOBEN walks along the path and puts her knitting back on the garden seat as the procession approaches her. BUTCH and BUDDY, GLORIA, CARSON and OULIOTTA stand on the steps with the mysterious RUSSIAN in the background.

W. C. FIELDS off: *Just wait a bit, folks.*

FIELDS comes up to MRS HEMOGLOBEN and takes off his hat.

W. C. FIELDS: *My dear Mrs Hemogloben . . .*

He offers her one perfect flower.

W. C. FIELDS : *A token of my love and esteem.*

As she sniffs the flower, she finds it has no head. FIELDS speaks sternly to the parrot.

W. C. FIELDS : *What a voracious appetite that little bird has.* He hands over the rest of the flowers.

W. C. FIELDS : *Oh, here they are.*

MRS HEMOGLOBEN : *Oh, thank you.*

FIELDS tosses the parrot away, then sits beside her.

W. C. FIELDS : *Fly away. He'll stay away. May I?*

MRS HEMOGLOBEN : *Oh, please do.*

As FIELDS sits down on the knitting bag on the seat, she chuckles and sits beside him. FIELDS is struggling to pull a knitting needle from his nether anatomy.

MRS HEMOGLOBEN : *Oh dear, are you hurt?*

W. C. FIELDS : *I can't tell yet.*

MRS HEMOGLOBEN : *Oh . . . my . . . oh . . .*

W. C. FIELDS : *Pardon me . . . may I remove the basket?*

He pulls out the sharp point, puts his hat on the bench, and sets aside the knitting bag. In the confusion, MRS HEMO-GLOBEN sits on his hat.

MRS HEMOGLOBEN : *Yes. Please do. Good gracious!*

W. C. FIELDS : *Yes.*

MRS HEMOGLOBEN : *My, oh my . . . I'm so sorry.*

FIELDS pulls out the squashed hat from beneath the lady.

W. C. FIELDS : *It's quite all right . . . it's quite all right.*

MRS HEMOGLOBEN : *Can you do anything with it?*

W. C. FIELDS : *I think I can do something with it. I don't know what yet.*

GLORIA and the two boys watch. She shakes her head.

GLORIA : *My Uncle Bill . . . but I still love him.*

W. C. FIELDS off : *My dear Mrs. Hemogloben . . .*

On the bench, FIELDS is in full flow of flattery.

W. C. FIELDS : *When I first saw you, I was so enamoured with your beauty . . .*

MRS HEMOGLOBEN : *Oh, Mr Fields . . .*

W. C. FIELDS : *I ran to the basket and jumped in . . . went down to the city and bought myself a wedding outfit . . .*

MRS HEMOGLOBEN giggles, edging down the seat towards him.

W. C. FIELDS : *And now I am here to lay my heart at your feet.*

MRS HEMOGLOBEN: *Oh . . . you're so full of romance.*

The seat begins to tip up, forcing her to rise.

W. C. FIELDS: *Every night . . . every night . . .*

He lands on the ground

W. C. FIELDS: *What's the matter with this . . . this? Sit down here again, will you?*

MRS HEMOGLOBEN helps him up.

MRS HEMOGLOBEN: *Yes. Let me help you up. Oh dear, everything seems to be going wrong.*

W. C. FIELDS: *Yes, it does.*

Standing by GLORIA, OULIOTTA sees her mother is in a receptive mood.

OULIOTTA: *Mother!*

She leads down CARSON with her to MRS HEMOGLOBEN and FIELDS.

OULIOTTA: *Mr Carson and I are going to be married and right away too. Mr Fields brought up the owner of the cantina . . . Mr Clines. He's the sheriff, the magistrate and mayor of the village. He's going to marry us immediately.*

W. C. FIELDS: *Why not make it a double-header . . . it's Saturday afternoon and I haven't anything to do.*

MRS HEMOGLOBEN: *Oh, Mr Fields . . . this is so sudden. Oh, I'm so happy.*

W. C. FIELDS: *So am I.*

Now LEON ERROL makes his entrance, running down the steps.

ERROL: *Hello there!*

All the people in the garden look at ERROL, including the RUSSIAN MAYOR, MAGISTRATE and CANTINA-OWNER, who runs off. ERROL takes MRS HEMOGLOBEN's hand.

ERROL: *Ah, my dream girl.*

FIELDS intervenes as ERROL embraces the protesting MRS HEMOGLOBEN and the two men end by embracing each other to laughter.

W. C. FIELDS: *Oh . . . ah, Leon, my rival . . . my pard . . . and me . . . Have you seen, er . . . my . . . er . . . her hanging swimming pool?*

ERROL: *No, I haven't.*

As the group in the garden stand watching, FIELDS takes his

trailing coat off and drops it before taking ERROL away.

W. C. FIELDS : *I'll show you the hanging swimming pool.*

The two rivals walk past a cypress tree in the garden until they reach the low wall on the edge of the precipice. They look over the drop.

ERROL : *Where is this hanging . . .*

W. C. FIELDS : *Why, right there. Get up on there and you can see a little better.*

ERROL hitches himself up on the wall.

ERROL : *Up here. Oh yeah.*

He is bending right over the wall, his back to us, when FIELDS gives him a push. He staggers, sways, tries to save himself.

ERROL : *Help! Help! Help!*

He clutches at a tall jar on the wall, but it does not save him from pitching over. There is a terrific musical crash.

FIELDS watches evilly, then steps up on the wall to look down, then finds himself side by side with the gorilla. He gasps and straightens up, raising his silk hat. The gorilla watches him. He bobs up and down. FIELDS starts to withdraw. He takes his whiskey-bottle out of his pocket and throws it over the edge.

W. C. FIELDS : *Sufferin' sciatica! Last time it was pink elephants.*

There is an explosion as the whiskey-bottle hits a rock, and FIELDS makes his escape.

Back in the garden, MRS HEMOGLOBEN and her daughter are seated with CARSON standing. FIELDS returns and puts on his wedding coat.

MRS HEMOGLOBEN : *Oh, you're back.*

W. C. FIELDS : *Yes. The poor chap just had a mishap.*

MRS HEMOGLOBEN : *That's too bad.*

W. C. FIELDS : *He slipped over the parapet.*

MRS HEMOGLOBEN : *Oh, my!*

W. C. FIELDS : *Shall we proceed with the ceremony?*

MRS HEMOGLOBEN : *Just as you say.*

W. C. FIELDS : *Thank you, Mrs Hemogloben.* He kisses her hand. *May I call you Daisy?*

MRS HEMOGLOBEN is ravished by this attention. GLORIA is looking hurt.

MRS HEMOGLOBEN : *Oh, I wish you would.*

GLORIA : *Uncle Bill.*

W. C. FIELDS : *Yes, dear.*

GLORIA : *May I see you a minute?*

W. C. FIELDS : *Certainly. Excuse me, Mrs Hemogloben.*

MRS HEMOGLOBEN : *Certainly.*

Seen from the top of the steps, GLORIA waits as FIELDS comes over to join her, while BUTCH and BUDDY and the RUSSIAN join CARSON and mother and daughter.

W. C. FIELDS : *What is it?*

GLORIA talks softly to her uncle.

GLORIA : *Uncle Bill, I don't want you to get married.*

W. C. FIELDS : *You listen to me, Missy! Don't you want to live in this beautiful nest? Have a personal maid?*

GLORIA : *No!*

W. C. FIELDS : *Wear diaphanous gowns and eat regularly?*

GLORIA : *I just want to be with you.*

W. C. FIELDS : *You'll be with me.*

GLORIA : *But she'll be with us.*

MRS HEMOGLOBEN sneers as she smells her bouquet.

Black on GLORIA with her uncle.

W. C. FIELDS : *I never thought of that.*

He walks off with GLORIA.

Uncle and niece come onto the high platform. She gets into the basket, while he turns the crank.

His hand releases the catch of the brake.

As the basket drops away, FIELDS dives into it with GLORIA and disappears. The handle whizzes round.

In the garden, the group rushes out.

In the basket, GLORIA is scared as it plunges down past the cliff-face.

GLORIA : *We're falling two thousand feet!*

W. C. FIELDS : *It's all right, dear. Don't start worrying until we get down one thousand, nine hundred and ninety-nine. It's the last foot that's dangerous.*

Cut back to MR PANGBORN's office, where he rises suddenly in fury and tries to tear the telephone book in half.

MR PANGBORN : *That's all! That's enough! That's too much! Airplanes with sundecks . . . Russian villages in the skies . . .*

66

gorillas playing post office . . . goat milk!

He starts to walk out.

FIELDS sits on the desk, disappointed.

MR PANGBORN off: *I'm going!*

Track with the raving MR PANGBORN as he crosses the office.

MR PANGBORN: *And when I get back, you'd better not be here.
I don't care where you go . . . just go! Go . . . get a drink . . .*

FIELDS stays on the desk.

MR PANGBORN off: *. . . Get two drinks! Get a dozen drinks!*

He goes out, slamming the door behind him.

Dissolve to an ice-cream parlor, where a MAN and a GIRL
are seated at a table. FIELDS comes in, looking hot and
bothered.

W. C. FIELDS: *Whew!*

The CLERK comes up to the end of the counter.

W. C. FIELDS: *Give me a drink. I'm dying.*

CLERK: *What'll it be?*

W. C. FIELDS: *Jumbo ice cream soda.*

CLERK: *What flavor?*

W. C. FIELDS: *Oh, I don't care. Spinach, horse-radish . . . anything you've got there.*

CLERK: *I'll give you peach.*

At the counter, FIELDS takes off his hat and tips us the wink.

W. C. FIELDS: *Oh, thank you, thank you. I feel as though somebody had stepped on my tongue with muddy feet. This scene
was supposed to be in a saloon, but the censor cut it out. It'll play
just as well.*

At the fountain, the CLERK prepares the soda. A fly bothers
him. FIELDS watches him from the counter.

W. C. FIELDS: *Oh, come on. Where's my drink?*

The CLERK puts down the soda, picks up a fly-swatter, and
prepares to swat.

W. C. FIELDS: *Hi-hi!*

Back at the counter, FIELDS grumbles.

W. C. FIELDS: *It's killers like you that give the West a bad name.
Give me a couple of lady-fingers, will you, please?*

The CLERK at the fountain tops up the soda with a chef's
hat of whipped cream, and plonks it down before FIELDS,

67

who tries to blow the cream off the glass.

The CLERK gets out of range behind the counter.

FIELDS picks up a couple of straws and injects them in the glass. He fishes for the cherry with the straws, gets it, loses it, gets it, loses it . . .

The CLERK watches and punches the cash register.

The NO SALE tab comes up in the register.

FIELDS is now fishing for his ice-cream and he isn't any angler. The straw bends, the ice plops back in the glass.

The CLERK is now watching the flies. He picks up a bottle to get them for good.

FIELDS goes on treating his soda like a booby-trap, while the CLERK watches. The straws keep on bending and letting him down.

W. C. FIELDS : *Ah, that's better . . .*

As the CLERK comes on, FIELDS leaves. The soda has beat him.

W. C. FIELDS : *So long, Tom. I'd rather be in a saloon at that.*

The CLERK leans on the counter, watching. He is startled to see . . .

The counter crawling with flies. He starts to strike with the bottle, then draws it back.

There is a fly crawling on his own face.

He hits himself with the bottle, breaks it and falls back in a daze.

Dissolve to MR PANGBORN'S office, where he is now holding onto GLORIA.

MR PANGBORN : *Don't you worry about it.*

GLORIA : *But Uncle Bill says he's going away.*

MR PANGBORN : *Fine! I mean . . . Now don't you worry about your Uncle Bill. He's lived his life . . . ruined mine. Now it's you we've got to think about. You're wrong. You've a great career ahead of you. You're going to do big things.*

GLORIA : *Maybe Uncle Bill can write you another story.*

MR PANGBORN is dismayed.

MR PANGBORN : *No, no. Don't say that. I never want to see him again. He's a numbskull.*

GLORIA : *You know what Uncle would do if he heard you say that?*

Mr Pangborn : *No. What would your uncle do if he heard me say that?*
Gloria : *This!* She slaps him. *And if Uncle Bill doesn't work here any more . . . I don't either.*
Track with Gloria as she walks out.

Dissolve to the interior of a jalopy, which Fields aims at driving with Gloria beside him.
Gloria : *But I don't want you to go away without me, Uncle Bill.*
W. C. Fields : *The enterprise on which I am about to embark upon is fraught with eminent peril. Much too dangerous for a young lady of your tender years. Another thing . . . I promised your mother I'd look out for you.*
Gloria grieves in close-up.
Gloria : *How can you look out for me when I'm here and you're away down there?*
Fields negotiates the wheel in close-up.
W. C. Fields : *You want to go to school, don't you?*
Now we see Gloria and Fields together talking.
Gloria : *No.*
W. C. Fields : *You want to grow up and be dumb like Zasu Pills?*
Gloria : *She only acts like that in pictures. I like her.*
W. C. Fields : *Don't you want to be smart?*
Gloria : *No. I want to be like you.*
W. C. Fields : *Don't you think I'm smart?*
Gloria : *Not very. I don't like teachers, anyhow.*
Fields again parleys with the wheel.
W. C. Fields : *No sense in arguing with a woman.*
Gloria looks off at him.
W. C. Fields off : *You go with me.*
Gloria : *Yippee!*
Delighted, she throws her arms about him. His hat falls off.
W. C. Fields : *Look out there!*
With a squeal of tires, Fields' car bumps against a police car parked at the kerb. The Police Officers inside look back, while other cars pass.
Fields is beserk in his car. He does not see that it is the police.
W. C. Fields : *Who do you think you're backing into, you big lummox!*

The two POLICE OFFICERS glare back from their car.

FIELDS laughs nervously.

W. C. FIELDS : *Hello, officer.* To GLORIA. *Here's a dollar and a quarter.* He indicates a women's store. *Go in there and buy yourself several outfits. We're liable to be down there a year.*

GLORIA : *Thank you.*

She gets out of the car and goes.

A POLICE OFFICER gets out of the police car and approaches FIELDS.

We now see that he is by a fire plug.

W. C. FIELDS : *Hello, officer. Am I too near the plug or something?*

The OFFICER stands by the car, ready to book FIELDS for ever.

W. C. FIELDS : *I can move out in a minute . . . move out in a minute.*

VOICE ON RADIO : *Calling Car Number 202. . . Calling Car Number 202 . . .*

The OFFICER walks back to the police car, gets in.

VOICE ON RADIO : *Go immediately to . . .*

FIELDS leaves his car for the police car, where the two OFFICERS sit, listening to the radio. He will not be left out.

VOICE ON RADIO : *Go immediately to North National Bank. Get necessary information regarding two crooks who have just held up the bank for a hundred and fifty thousand dollars. One hundred and fifty thousand. That is all.*

W. C. FIELDS : *That is all! A hundred and fifty thousand dollars ain't hay, is it?*

VOICE ON RADIO : *Car 202 . . . bank robbery. North National Bank has been held up. One crook slight build . . . evidently a jockey . . . has a horse scar behind his left ear.*

W. C. FIELDS : *Must be some ear to get a horse car behind it.*

POLICE OFFICER : *Keep quiet, please.*

VOICE ON RADIO : *Other crook has corn teeth, cauliflower ear, apple-red cheeks . . . mutton-chop whiskers . . .*

W. C. FIELDS : *Sounds like a four course dinner to me. What, no apple pie?*

One of the POLICE OFFICERS is really angry.

POLICE OFFICER : *Oh, shut up!*

The police car starts up and moves off, leaving FIELDS looking wistfully after it. Outside the women's store, GLORIA stands with the DOORMAN. She starts inside.

By a showcase, a plump woman, MRS WILSON is talking with a CLERK as she looks at baby things, then catches sight of the store clock.

MRS WILSON: *Now it's blue for a boy and pink for a girl, isn't it?*

CLERK: *Yes.*

MRS WILSON: *Well, I'll take the pink one. Is that the right time?*

CLERK: *Yes. It's Western Postal Time.*

MRS WILSON: *I have to get these down to the Baby Hospital. I'm leaving for Salt Lake this afternoon. Here . . . I'll see you when I get back.*

CLERK: *All right, Mrs Wilson.*

She hands some money to the CLERK, picks up a blanket and goes out. By the entrance door of the store, the DOORMAN stands with FIELDS in his car at the kerb. As MRS WILSON hurries out, the DOORMAN whistles.

FIELDS looks up from his car.

MRS WILSON speaks to the DOORMAN, who looks down at the blanket she is holding.

MRS WILSON: *I've got to get to the Maternity Hospital right away.*

Scenting action, FIELDS calls out from his car.

W. C. FIELDS: *If I can be of any assistance?*

Seen from the entrance door, the DOORMAN hands MRS WILSON into FIELDS' car.

DOORMAN: *This lady has to get to the Maternity Hospital.*

W. C. FIELDS: *Yes, sir. Get her in the back.*

FIELDS jerks his car into action.

W. C. FIELDS: *And . . . tell my niece . . .*

The car shoots off.

W. C. FIELDS off: *To meet me at the . . .*

DOORMAN: *I'll take care of her, sir.*

There is general traffic in the wholesale district.

The camera pulls back as FIELDS' sedan car squeals round the corner, dodges other cars, and goes up onto the sidewalk. FIELDS drives on imperturbably, whilst MRS WILSON in the rear seat knocks on the glass partition between them, shouting inaudibly.

FIELDS' foot presses down on the accelerator.

Now we are inside the moving car behind FIELDS and MRS

71

WILSON. Through the windshield, we see his car dodge other cars as MRS WILSON knocks on the partition with her umbrella.

MRS WILSON: *Slow down! Take it easy, will you, please?*

Now we are in front with FIELDS driving and the terrified MRS WILSON back of the glass partition.

W. C. FIELDS: *I can't get it down any further. It's all I can get out of this old crate.*

Now behind FIELDS, we see through the windshield the car dodging through the traffic at high speed.

Back of the glass, MRS WILSON screams, faints, and falls over. FIELDS drives furiously among the other cars. He looks back. MRS WILSON has passed out on the rear seat.

FIELDS looks about in the driver's seat.

Camera moves back and round by the entrance to an under-pass, as FIELDS' sedan dashes over a cross street against the traffic and squeals off, leaving a COP frantic at the intersection. In a suburban business street, the traffic bumbles along, except for FIELDS' buggy, proceeding furiously and braking.

The rear end of the sedan car erupts in clouds and smoke. It backs at a street corner, meets another car, backs up. Two cars coming towards the backing sedan separate to avoid it, then nearly collide once they are past.

One of the cars runs onto the sidewalk, while a roadster crashes into the second car.

FIELDS' backing buggy nearly hits a dodging TRAFFIC COP, then comes to a halt, as traffic whizzes by in all directions. FIELDS points to the unconscious woman in the back seat.

W. C. FIELDS: *To the Maternity Hospital.*

COP: *Fourteenth and B street.*

He leaps onto the running board of FIELDS' sedan.

The sedan turns towards us, avoids other cars, squeals off. Now we are in a warehouse district with trucks loading and cars passing As the COP rides the running-board of FIELDS' sedan, it almost hits a telephone pole, swings past the obstacle, and away.

In another street, a passing truck nearly shaves off the COP's leg.

Two trucks now charge the sedan, which goes so close that

the seat of the Cop's pants is torn off.

A bus begins to turn round a street corner, as we pan with it. The sedan charges it with the Cop hanging on for dear life. Near as a whisker, Fields gets by and drives across the street. The Cop is left behind, hanging from the bus. The startled driver and passengers lean out to clutch him safe. Pedestrians crossing the street look off in horror.

The sedan crosses at speed in and out of parked trucks.

The scared pedestrians scream and leap off in all directions, leaving their shoes behind.

Outside a warehouse, two motor-cycle Cops turn in circles and start back up a side street.

Below an elevated highway, cars are parked with other cars passing. The sedan charges in and out, almost meeting another car. Its driver falls out, gets up and runs forwards.

Fields at the wheel looks back.

Mrs Wilson is still unconscious in the rear seat.

The anxious Fields turns back to the road.

As the driver of the wrecked car stands by it, the motorcycle Cops roar past him. He is whisked round, and he falls. More cars and trucks are parked in a street where the sedan charges along followed by the motor-cycle Cops. Seen from a camera car, the two Cops overtake the Fields' buggy, and pull up beside it.

One of the Cops yells across to Fields.

Cop: *Where do you think you're going to—a fire?*

W. C. Fields: *Er . . .*

He points back at the unconscious woman on the back seat.

W. C. Fields off: *Paternity Hospital.*

The Cop on his motorcycle nods.

Cop: *O.K. Follow me.*

Now the two speed Cops escort Fields instead of chasing him. Traffic on the cross streets stops for them, as the sirens blast off.

Back of Fields in the moving car, we see the speed Cops through the windshield as they lead the way through the traffic. As they turn a corner, the sunshield drops down. Fields tries to adjust it.

The two speed Cops and the sedan hurtle up a street.

73

In the car, FIELDS is having more trouble with the sunshield. He tears it off. As he does so, the second sunshield swings across to blind him. While the speed COPS turn another corner, FIELDS tears the second shield loose and throws it away, as they reach the freeway.

In the back seat, the unconscious MRS WILSON is being shaken by the jerking springs.

One of the COPS drops back beside FIELDS.

W. C. FIELDS : *Short cut to the hospital!*

As he extends his arm to signal, he hits the COP in the face. Now on the freeway with traffic in all the lanes, the two speed COPS lead the sedan off onto a steep hillside road.

Cut to a sign on the freeway : ONE WAY TUNNEL.

KEEP TO THE RIGHT

The two COPS and the FIELDS' buggy are circling round the exit road. The sedan goes over the kerb, and just misses an oncoming car, then crosses over the road with the COPS following. Pan with the sedan to a high bridge and tunnel entrance, where FIELDS is leading us into the gun's mouth. A car coming up the tunnel dodges round the sedan and the COPS, as they charge in. They vanish, and out comes an open car with its front wheel and fender stove in. It crashes into a side wall.

Hooting comes out of the far end of the tunnel as the FIELDS' buggy and one COP scream out, dodging the oncoming traffic.

At this end of the tunnel, one car is smashed against the wall at the side, while another comes out with the second COP and his motorcycle draped over its hood. It stops and the driver gets out, overcome.

In another street, we pan with the sedan and the surviving COP as they jink past a bus.

Now we shoot past cars parked along the kerb and stopped to let a fire truck scream by.

A street crossing is seen from above, as the fire truck shoots across with FIELDS' buggy and the surviving COP swerving round the fire truck, then racing along with it. Pan with them as they wash other traffic to right and left like a bow-wave, then move back as they turn down a street at full throttle.

FIELDS, driving furiously, sounds his horn to add to the screaming of the sirens.

On the back of the fire truck, the TILLER FIREMAN at the rear steering-wheel looks back and points off.

Now in a general shot we see the TILLER FIREMAN making signs behind. The sedan swings to the rear of the fire truck. The hooks on the end of the fire-ladder catch the top of FIELDS' buggy which begins dragging out the extending ladder. As the ladder extends, the TILLER FIREMAN is dragged off with it.

Again from the back of the truck, we see the ladder hooked onto FIELDS' buggy, pulling it along behind the fire truck, with the motorcycle COP in hot pursuit. The TILLER FIREMAN is waving his arms frantically.

On the moving ladder, the FIREMAN does gymnastics round the rungs. He swings down below his seat on the truck.

In the sedan, FIELDS sits at the wheel, his back to us.

Through the windshield, we see the FIREMAN upside-down in front of the car, suspended from the ladder.

W. C. FIELDS : *Darn those drunken painters!*

FIELDS pounds on the horn button as he drives, then looks off. The horn on a long coil spring swings up and hits him in the face. Desperately he tries to push it back.

On the moving ladder, the FIREMAN does acrobatics round his seat and manages to get back on it.

On a bridge near, we see the rear part of the fire truck with its TILLER FIREMAN trying to unhook the FIELDS' buggy, and the motorcycle cop tagging on behind.

In a street, two couples in an open car look back, startled at the screaming sirens. Ahead of them more cars.

Through the traffic, the fire truck screams, dragging the sedan with it and the COP after it.

The two couples in the open car duck down and the car shoots off, driverless.

The fire truck and company swerve into a side street.

Cautiously the couples in the open car now emerge from the bonnet of the car.

Down a boulevard, the fire truck races with the sedan swinging right and left behind it at the end of the ladder, and the COP in pursuit. All shoot under a bridge, below us. The bucketing sedan shakes behind the fire-truck.

FIELDS clings to the wheel like a grounded lifebelt.

We are now above an underpass, with the firetruck shooting away, the TILLER FIREMAN trying to disengage the sedan and keep on the ladder, and the COP bringing up the rear. Another car coming down a grade seems bound to crash into the truck, but shoots through the gap under the ladder between the truck and the sedan. The camera rises now to show a long bridge over a river. The sedan whiplashes across the street at the back of the truck, and another car squeaks through the gap under the ladder.

Back inside the car, FIELDS holds the wheel as he zigzags at furious speed. The wheel comes loose.

W. C. FIELDS: *Whoa!*

The FIREMAN does Olympic gymnastics on the ladder.

FIELDS waves the FIREMEN out of the way and the wheel hits him in the face.

W. C. FIELDS: *Look out there!*

The fire truck screams across the bridge, pulling along the sedan on the extension ladder with the COP tailing. The FIREMAN gets back to his seat. Pan to show the distant city beyond.

In the car, the steering wheel comes loose in FIELDS' hand.

W. C. FIELDS: *Get out of there!*

The fire truck approaches two roads, one going beneath an underpass. As the truck takes the low road, the sedan takes the high road. Pan to show the ladder passing over another car, as FIELDS rises and the fire truck goes down to hell.

In the truck, the FIREMEN at the ladder controls looks up and pulls a lever.

FIELDS at the wheel is startled as his buggy takes off.

Now we see the car lifted off the upper ramp by the extension ladder and swung across.

FIELDS looks down, unperturbed.

W. C. FIELDS: *What a splendid view of the California climate!*

The car is lowered down by the extension ladder to the lower ramp.

FIELDS bounces up and down as his sedan hits the tarmac.

By the front part of the fire truck, the motor Cop has drawn level and is yelling to the two FIREMEN in the front seats.

The two FIREMEN in front are surprised.

FIREMAN: *He says the fire's back there!*

Shot from above, we see the fire truck spin round, with the FIELDS' buggy whiplashing at the end of the ladder and cops scattering like flies.

The sedan plunges towards the side of the street.

FIELDS at the loose wheel looks off in fear.

The motorcycle Cop, still up front, yells to the two FIREMEN.

COP: *Back! Back! Look back!*

The two FIREMEN don't like this.

FIREMAN: *Tell him to make up his mind!*

The fire truck does another turn about down a tree-shaded street with the FIELDS' buggy again whiplashing through the scattering traffic.

FIELDS still clings to his broken wheel.

Track with the swinging sedan as the end of the exterior ladder breaks loose from the car, then pan across to a sign:

MATERNITY HOSPITAL

QUIET

The car disappears behind the sign and there is a tremendous crash . . .

Outside the hospital, FIELDS begins to rise out of his wrecked car. The door falls off and he carries the steering wheel in his hand.

W. C. FIELDS: *Stretcher!*

Two ATTENDANTS run forward with a hospital cart. Pan with them to show the street scene.

Among the wreckage, FIELDS struggles, delivering the goods to the two hospital men.

Dissolve to a hospital corridor, where MRS WILSON is being trundled along on the cart, surrounded by NURSES.

She suddenly sits up and screams, while a NURSE tries to hush her. The cart stops.

NURSE: *Quiet, please.*

MRS WILSON: *Where am I?*

NURSE: *Quiet, please. You'll alarm the other patients.*

MRS WILSON pushes and struggles with an INTERN, trying to

get off the cart.

MRS WILSON: *What do I care about the other patients? Where are my clothes? Get away from me!*

INTERN: *But, madam, just a minute!*

MRS WILSON: *Just a minute, nothing! You give me my clothes and let me out of here.*

She gets off the cart and rushes off, pursued by the NURSE and the two INTERNS.

Outside the building, a cab pulls up in a squeal of brakes with GLORIA inside. She looks out.

GLORIA calling: *Uncle Bill! Are you all right?*

FIELDS is still extricating himself from his wrecked car.

W. C. FIELDS: *Lucky I didn't have an accident, or I'd never have gotten here.*

GLORIA looks out wistfully from the cab window.

GLORIA: *My Uncle Bill! But I still love him.*

Music starts up as we fade out to THE END.

TILLIE AND GUS

Tillie and Gus

CREDITS:

Directed by	Francis Martin
Production company	Paramount Productions Inc.
Screenplay	Walter Deleon and
	Francis Martin
Adapted from a story by	Rupert Hughes
Photography	Ben Reynolds
Art direction	Hans Dreier
	Harry Oliver
Running time	58 minutes
First shown	1933

CAST:

Augustus Winterbottom	W. C. Fields
Tillie Winterbottom	Alison Skipworth
The 'King'	Baby LeRoy
Mary Sheridan	Jacqueline Wells
Tom Sheridan	Clifford Jones
Phineas Pratt	Clarence Wilson
Captain Fogg	George Barbier
Commissioner McLennan	Barton MacLane
Judge	Edgar Kennedy
Defense Attorney	Robert McKenzie
The Swede	Ivan Linow
High-Card Harrington	Master Williams

Outside a pleasant house, a goose quacks as it goes up the path with the camera following it.

The goose wipes its feet on the mat before the front door, which is open. Then it goes into the house, quacking. We follow the noisy goose as it foots it into the living room, where a charming young couple, MARY and TOM SHERIDAN, are sitting with the smiling villain PHINEAS PRATT, who has a spread of legal papers with him on a table.

PRATT : *You're right, Mary. He was a good father and a generous friend, but a terrible businessman.*

Mary looks up in trust.

PRATT off : *Yes, sir, just no business sense at all.*

MARY : *But what about all the property Dad owned?*

Back close to the three in conference.

PRATT : *Mortgaged to the hilt, all of it. Here. You can see the figures for yourself.*

Unable to figure out anything, the young couple look at PRATT's papers.

PRATT : *I've been a-workin' on 'em ever since John died. Yes, sir! I've been executor of many an estate . . .*

TOM : *But surely there must be something left of the estate?*

PRATT : *Nothin' that ain't swallowed up by debts. Now, about that money you loaned the estate . . .*

TOM is embarrassed in front of MARY's look.

TOM : *Uh . . . to help with the immediate expenses, honey . . . the . . . funeral. I didn't want you bothered.*

PRATT off : *Eleven hundred and forty-three dollars.*

MARY : *Eleven hundred! Why, that's all the money you had to finish college.*

TOM : *Now, don't get excited, honey.*

MARY : *But that means you won't get your engineer's degree.*

TOM : *Well . . . well, a married man has no business going to college, anyway.*

MARY to Pratt : *You had no right to take it!*

PRATT explains himself.

PRATT: *It's been a-worryin' me too. Yes, sir! Started me schemin' a way to help you. Now there's one item I ain't mentioned, because . . . well, it's more of a liability than an asset. Your father's ferry-boat.*

TOM is on his guard beside MARY.

TOM: *And the franchise to operate the ferry line.*

PRATT is talking too quickly.

PRATT: *Don't mean nothin'. The old Fairy Queen's been laid up for weeks. But . . . uh . . . seein' as you both need cash . . . heh . . . well, it ain't business, but I'll give you four hundred dollars for it.*

As he pounds the desk, TOM intervenes, rising to his feet.

TOM: *Thanks, Mr Pratt, but I'm sure Mary doesn't want to sell.*

MARY: *Why not, Tom?*

TOM: *No, honey. We . . .*

The goose—obviously a Roman watchdog goose—quacks its warning.

PRATT: *Well, you're bein' foolish, young man.*

The goose quacks again.

Cut back to the group, now standing. MARY admonishes the goose.

MARY: *Quiet, Doc.*

PRATT: *You're goin' to need money for food and rent.*

MARY: *Rent? Why, we still have the old home here.*

PRATT: *Well, I was a-comin' to that. You see, there was a mortgage . . .*

MARY: *A mortgage? Do you mean we've lost it . . . the home my great grand-daddy built?*

PRATT: *Well, knowin' you wouldn't want a stranger to get it, I bought it myself, house and furniture. Cost me more than it's worth, but . . . well, your father was my friend.*

MARY: *But I . . . I was born here. I've never lived anywhere else.*

TOM: *Mr. Pratt, you're not asking Mary to move out, are you?*

PRATT: *No hurry. Take your time. I won't be movin' in till next Thursday. Well, I've done the best I could with an ornery job, and I'm glad it's over. Yes, sir! And to show you how bad I feel about it, I'll give you five hundred for the old ferry line.*

TOM: *No, thank you.*

81

PRATT: *You're a young fool.*

Doc the goose quacks and tears the lining out of PRATT's hat and throws it on the floor.

Back on the trio, we pan down to the goose's revenge.

TOM: *Take it easy!*

PRATT rescuing his hat: *Mary, think it over. It's your boat, you know. Good day.* He leaves.

MARY: *Why didn't you let him buy the boat?*

TOM is now beside MARY.

TOM: *Because Phineas Pratt is a crook and because I have an idea. I'm an engineer . . . well, almost. I'll put that old crate back in service and make a fortune!*

Doc the goose quacks his approval.

MARY: *Do you really think so?*

TOM: *Well, anyway, a living.* He laughs.

MARY: *Oh! Tom!*

Her attention is caught by a family portrait.

MARY off: *Aunt Tillie and Uncle Gus.*

The faces of W. C. Fields and Alison Skipworth—Augustus ('Gus') and Tillie Winterbottom—stare at us from a photograph. They are dressed in unlikely respectability.

Back to MARY and TOM.

TOM: *Oh, you mean the missionaries?*

MARY: *Yes, how terrible!*

TOM: *Well, what's terrible about missionaries?*

MARY: *They were notified a month ago to come here for their share of the estate.*

TOM: *Oh, say, that's too bad. Can't we stop them?*

MARY: *It's too late now. What a shame, dragging Aunt Tillie from her missionary work, all the way from China.*

TOM: *Well, how about your Uncle Gus coming all the way from Alaska? Huh! That's no street car ride.*

MARY: *Imagine the old dears travelling thousands of miles, for nothing.*

There is the cry of a baby. The parents look up.

TOM: *The King! He's waked up.*

MARY: *The little darling.*

Tom and Mary hurry off, before THE KING gets into full cry. Now in the hall of the house we see Mary and Tom running up the stairs to the baby's cry.

They rush into the bedroom to see.

Baby LeRoy, alias THE KING covered with feathers from his wrecked pillow, which he throws to the floor from his cradle.

KING : *Boo!*

MARY and TOM laugh with delight and relief.

TOM : *The little darling!*

TOM picks up the gurgling baby and plays with him.

TOM : *Whew! Wee!*

KING : *Ooh!*

TOM laughing : *Here.*

As he hands his son to MARY, we fade out on this scene of domestic bliss.

Fade in to a close-up of the soles of a pair of hobnailed boots, labelled Joe's Emporium, Lone Gulch, Alaska, then tilt up to a rough group of bandits, who look like they are in jail, only they happen to be in the jury box.

ATTORNEY off : *Gentlemen of the jury! Gaze on the defendant! Have you even seen a countenance so honest, so open, so innocent . . .*

As the ATTORNEY talks, we move from mug to mug of the wanted men on the jury until we end on the FOREMAN whittling the rail. The ATTORNEY is trying to jerk a tear.

ATTORNEY : *. . . as the face of this persecuted . . .*

Gus's sly look cannot help the defence.

ATTORNEY off : *. . . defendant, Augustus Q. Winterbottom?*

One of the jurors has to speak out.

JUROR : *He'd steal anything that wouldn't bite him.*

Gus fails to look injured or innocent.

The FOREMAN is getting impatient among the jurors.

FOREMAN : *Judge, is there any sense of goin' on with this here trial?*

The JUDGE pronounces.

JUDGE : *This is a court of justice and according to law we ought to try him a while before we hang him.*

Gus looks uneasy.

His hand palms a coin.

He looks up again at the sound of the gavel.

JUDGE off : *The defendant will take the stand.*

As he takes his place in the witness stand, Gus strikes a match for his cheroot on a man's back on the way. Pan with him as he gets up to tell the JUDGE nothing of the truth.

The JUDGE looks at him sternly.

JUDGE : *I suppose you're acquainted with the penalty for perjury?*

Gus won't have that.

GUS : *I object!*

The JUDGE grabs the gavel and bangs it down. It misses Gus's hand by an inch or so.

JUDGE : *Objection over-ruled! Sit down!*

Gus puts his hat on the JUDGE's desk.

The JUDGE throws the hat on the floor.

JUDGE : *Gus, you are hereby charged . . .*

Gus listens to the indictment.

JUDGE off : *. . . with pumping a load of lead into the anatomy of one High-Card Harrington.*

The bandaged HIGH-CARD HARRINGTON puts in his bit, his crutch by his seat.

HIGH-CARD : *Six shots!*

The JUDGE clarifies.

JUDGE : *Six hits!*

Gus takes a bottle out of his pocket.

GUS : *Six cigars!*

The JUDGE licks his lips.

Gus takes a drink.

The JUDGE looks thirsty.

Gus lowers the bottle.

To put out the fire inside, Gus drinks some water from the JUDGE's pitcher, then throws the rest of the water behind the desk.

GUS : *You shoulda worn your goloshes.*

The JUDGE has the last word as he leans towards the accused.

JUDGE : *Have you anything more to say before I find you guilty?*

GUS : *So you're goin' to deal from a cold deck, eh?*

Pan onto Gus as he rises to his defence.

GUS : *Boys, this mummy . . .*

HIGH-CARD HARRINGTON is not amused.

GUS off : *. . . sitting over here inveigled me into a game of chance entitled . . .*

Gus warms to his brief.

GUS: *. . . draw poker. I figured right from the start I'd have to shoot him. It was all I could do to take his money!*

The jury is sympathetic.

FOREMAN: *Know just how you felt.*

HIGH-CARD HARRINGTON is unbelieving.

HIGH-CARD: *What a country!*

Gus sits, his defence concluded.

Move along the feet of the jury in their boots, leaning against the rail as the foreman's hand whittles at the wood.

Gus watches as there is a crash and laughter.

The rail has broken and the jurors are all swearing and sprawling on the floor.

The JUDGE gives a ruling beside GUS.

JUDGE: *You fellows gotta quit skylarkin' or go outside.*

GUS: *That's telling' 'em, Elmer . . . Your Honor . . . old naked-skull . . . old boy.* To jury. *Now listen, you . . . gentlemen of the jury . . .*

Gus is in full flow again.

GUS: *In this here game with High-Card, gents, I deals myself four aces, all regular. What is my astonishment when High-Card there lays down five aces, against my four!*

The JUDGE is shocked.

GUS off: *I'm a broadminded man, gents.*

Gus is high and righteous.

GUS: *I don't object to nine aces in one deck, but when a man lays down five aces in one hand . . . ! And, besides, I know what I dealt him.*

The jury thinks it is a bum deal.

The JUDGE, however, wants to clear the court, so he tells GUS:

JUDGE: *Gus, it is the judgement of this Court that your cards has too many aces in the deck . . .*

Gus can't believe his ears.

JUDGE off: *. . . So this Court rules that the citizens ain't to start . . .*

The JUDGE shows his mercy.

JUDGE: *. . . shootin' at you for one hour and a half, specific standard time. Get goin'!*

The crowded courtroom breaks up in disorder as the crowd breaks up the courtroom.

Dissolve to the interior of a log cabin, where the coughing GUS is packing his high silk hat in a suitcase, watched by the old prospector SOURDOUGH.

SOURDOUGH: *Handsome, whyn't you ever thought of marryin' and settlin' down?*

GUS: *I was married once, to a saintly woman if ever there was one! She threw a forty-four slug into my right shoulder. She was a woman of impulse. She's a missionary now in China, doing noble work among the lowly heathen.*

SOURDOUGH: *Well, I'll be dad-blamed.*

GUS opens a letter to him as if it were a grenade, and reads it.

GUS: *'Mr. Augustus Q. Winterbottom. Dear Sir: The last will and testament of the late . . .'*

Now we see the letter in close-up, addressed to Augustus Q. Winterbottom, Lone Gulch, Alaska.

GUS off: *'John Blake, includes you among the beanfisheries. Your presence in Danville will facilitate the distribution of said large estate.'*

GUS finishes reading the letter.

GUS: *'Yours truly, Phineas Pratt, executor.'*

SOURDOUGH is impressed.

SOURDOUGH: *Well, I'll be dad-blamed!*

GUS: *And now the poor fellow's in a moratorium.*

GUS tucks the letter into his pocket and crosses the room to the door, ready for a grand adieu.

GUS: *There comes a time in the affairs of men, my dear Blubber, when we must take the bull by the tail and face the situation.*

Fade out and fade in to a Chinese street scene where some characters are passing, then move up to a sign:

SOO CHOW
CLUB

TILLIE WINTERBOTTOM: Proprietor.

Now pan to some swing-doors through which a MAN is pushing his way in.

There is the noise of voices and a honky-tonk piano.

Inside the club, people sit at the tables. The MAN who has come in goes up to a WAITER.

MAN: *How's Tillie doin' with the dice?*

WAITER : *She's been losing steady since midnight.*
BARTENDER off : *Here, for the Professor.*

> He gives a drink to the WAITER, who carries it over to the
> PIANIST.

WAITER : *Here you are, Professor.*

> The PIANIST stops playing to gargle.

PIANIST : *Oh, thanks. I hear Tillie's in bad shape.*
WAITER off : *Yeah, looks like the old girl is pretty near through.*
PIANIST : *Too bad. I've never worked for any woman, East or West,
that looked out for the Professor the way Tillie does.*

> A group of people is bunched round a dice table. To the click
> of the bones and murmur of voices, we move up to Alison
> Skipworth, alias TILLIE, who is playing dice with a SWEDE.
> As the dice roll, we hear a man cry.

MAN off : *Velvet!*
CHINAMAN : *Ten straight passes!*

> Now we look down on the dice game.

SWEDE : *This time, Tillie, I shoot ten thousand.*
TILLIE : *Dragging down, eh? Well, Swede . . .* She laughs . . .
Just to be sociable . . . I shall fade you.

> She throws a piece of paper on the table.

SWEDE : *What's that?*
TILLIE : *That . . .* She laughs . . . *my dear Swede, that is a judgement against my ex-husband, Gus Winterbottom, for ten thousand
dollars alimony.*

> A MESSENGER BOY comes on and gives TILLIE a letter.

BOY : *This for you, madam.*
TILLIE : *Huh?* She opens the letter. *Well, it can't be any worse
than the bad news I've been reading on the dice.*

> Again we see the same letter that GUS received, only it is
> addressed this time to Tillie Winterbottom, Soo Chow Club,
> Shanghai, China.
> A MAN is reading the letter with TILLIE at the dice table.

MAN : *Well, Tillie, it looks like you hauled off and got lucky again.*
TILLIE : *Yes. My poor brother!*
MAN : *Who's this fellow, Phineas Pratt?*
TILLIE : *A crook, an old friend of the family. I've known him since
we were children. We went to school toget . . . I trust you've
finished.*

She turns round to the group at the table.

TILLIE: *Boys, I've got to take the first steamer back to the States.*

She has a last throw against the SWEDE.

TILLIE: *Swede, what will you shoot against the joint . . . lease, lock, layouts and liquor?*

SWEDE: *Twenty thousand.*

TILLIE: *Good! It's about time the Big Swede crapped.*

The SWEDE throws.

The dice fall, seven up.

TILLIE rises slowly and considers the SWEDE.

TILLIE: No complaints, Swede, of course, but who made your dice *for you?*

SWEDE: *A fellow in Alaska, called Gus Winterbottom.*

TILLIE: *At the first opportunity, I must shoot that ex-husband of mine, personally. Good-bye, boys.*

Fade out and fade in to a railroad station, marked SEATTLE. Then dissolve on the sound of train noises to a general shot of passengers on the platform before dissolving to a sign inside the station: MEN'S SMOKING ROOM. Again there are voices and the rattle of dice as we pan down to some men seated on a bench, playing dice rolled by GUS, who is gathering in the money from the suckers.

GUS: *Give me that money.* He sings. *Bringing in the sheaves/ Bringing in the sheaves/We will come rejoicing . . . A hundred and twenty, a hundred and twenty-five, a hundred and thirty . . .*

Now we move with GUS across to the ticket-clerk at his window. GUS taps the shoulder of the man waiting at the head of the queue for tickets. As the man turns around, GUS steps into his place and speaks to the CLERK.

GUS: *Got that berth to Danville?*

CLERK: *Lower Eight, Car Seventy-five . . .* GUS grunts . . . *A hundred and forty dollars, please.*

GUS: *A hundred and forty? I though you said a hundred and thirty-five.*

CLERK: *One hundred and forty!*

GUS: *No matter, no matter. What man has done, man can do. Pardon me.*

He goes off to bring in more sheaves.

In another part of the station, TILLIE is sitting at a table with a WOMAN, who looks rather official.

WOMAN: *Mrs Mathilda Winterbottom. You say you're a Chinese missionary?*

TILLIE: *I said I was a missionary in China, and that, I understand, entitles me to a reduction in railroad fare.*

WOMAN: *Of course. How did you conduct your work?*

TILLIE: *Through kindness. My object was to bring them in out of the darkness, to put more spirits into them . . . uh . . . as it were, and relieve them of their material burdens.*

WOMAN: *How interesting! Sign here, please.* TILLIE signs. *Oh, while you were over there, did you have any Chinese children?*

TILLIE is taken aback.

WOMAN: *Oh! I mean Chinese children in the Mission!*

TILLIE with a cool nod: *Oh!*

WOMAN: *Well, just present this to the ticket agent. It entitles you to a ten per cent reduction.*

TILLIE: *I thank you.*

In another part of the station, GUS is coming back from the harvest.

GUS: *Bringing in the sheaves, Bringing in the sheaves . . .*

TILLIE is now at the ticket window with the clerk, as GUS comes in.

CLERK: *Berth Eight, Car Seventy-five.*

GUS: *Not so fast, you weed-bender. I reserved Berth Eight.*

TILLIE registers who he is.

GUS registers who TILLIE is.

TILLIE reaches in her bag for her gun, before her grateful ex-husband stops her.

GUS: *The passing years have slowed you on the draw, my little chickadee . . . Which way are you heading, my little dove?*

TILLIE puts back her gun in her bag again.

TILLIE: *Canada, possibly. What section of the country do you intend to ravish?*

GUS: *A sentimental journey to all . . .*

A SUCKER is passing in a fine tall silk hat. GUS knocks off the hat, and lets his own hat fall. Both now stoop for their head-gear and by the time they rise, GUS has traded his old hat and cane for the SUCKER's new ones.

GUS: *Please be careful, sir.*

SUCKER: *Well! I . . . I am sorry.*

GUS: *It's quite all right, quite all right. It's a pardonable sin.*

As the SUCKER goes, TILLIE sees that her old man has not lost his touch.

The CLERK hands out a ticket to GUS.

CLERK: *Your ticket to Danville, Doctor.*

GUS: *Oh!*

TILLIE: *Danville!*

CLERK: *That's your train also, madam. Track Six.*

GUARD off: *Sunkist Express. Salt Lake . . .*

TILLIE and GUS go off after their train.

On the platform, GUS and TILLIE approach the guard.

GUARD: *. . . Denver and points East.*

GUS: *We're not interested in which way it points.*

Now we dissolve to a compartment in the train, which whistles and rumbles. GUS and TILLIE make their plans.

TILLIE: *My brother was a very wealthy man . . . and there is but one heir beside us . . . my niece, a girl of twenty.*

GUS: *Wouldn't it be advisable for us to get ourselves appointed her guardians?*

TILLIE: *That is my intention.*

A gambler called MR. WHITE leans over the respectable couple, and clears his throat.

MR WHITE: *Pardon me, folks, we're starting a little game of poker. Would you care to play?*

GUS: *Poker?*

MR WHITE: *Um-hmm.*

GUS: *Is that the game where one receives five cards? And if there's two alike that's pretty good, but if there's three alike, that's much better?*

MR WHITE: *Oh, you'll learn the game in no time.*

GUS is very hopeful.

GUS: *Yes.*

TILLIE: *Yes. He picks things up very quickly.*

MR WHITE: *We're in the rear end—the next car.*

He turns away to his game.

GUS: *Crooked as a dog's hind leg. He's a wool in sheep's clothing.*

TILLIE: *Will you take them or shall I?*

90

Gus : *I will. You were always better at the galloping dominoes. Come on.*

As he gets up, we dissolve into another compartment, where Gus is now innocently holding a pack of cards with three gamblers about him, Mr. White, Mr. Black and Mr. Green.

Gus : Shall I distribute the cards?

Mr White : *The usual procedure is to cut for the deal. Goes to the one drawing the highest card.*

Mr. Black : *And the ace is high.*

Gus : *You must forgive the ignorance of a novice.*

Mr. Black laughs as the men cut the cards.

Mr White : *Queen.*

Mr Black : *Ten.*

As Mr. Green turns up a king, Gus shows his card at twice the speed of light.

Mr Green : *King.*

Gus : *Ace.*

Gus's card is back in the pack while still invisible. Mr. White and Mr. Black are not quite satisfied.

Mr. White politely : *Oh, I beg your pardon, Doctor, I'm afraid I didn't see that ace.*

Mr. Green was also unsighted beside Gus.

Mr. Green : *Nor I.*

Gus : *You saw it, didn't you?*

Mr. Black is not sure.

Mr. Black : *Why . . . uh . . . no . . . uh . . .*

Gus is apologetic. He begins running through the pack.

Gus : *Goodness gracious! Have I transgressed again?*

He finds an ace and produces it as proof.

Gus : *There it is!* He looks off, shuffling the cards expertly. *By the way, what was that exciting game we played on the ship coming over?*

Tillie is now standing behind Mr. White.

Tillie : *Casino. Don't you just love Casino, Mr White?*

Mr White : *I prefer pinochle.*

Gus is again ignorant, as he deals the cards like a professional, with too many for himself.

Gus : *Pinochle? That's the top of something, isn't it? The pinochle of a hill, for instance?*

Mr. Green : *That's enough. Five cards is all that's legal.*

Gus : *Thanks. I must remember that.*

More money is produced by the three gamblers.

Gus : *Fresh money! I'm shy for the minute.*

Tillie watches the play from behind the gamblers.

There is a pair of jacks in Mr. White's hand.

Tillie casually looks down at the faces of the cards.

Tillie : *By the way, I saw those two sailors off the ship today.*

Gus gets the tip as he sits beside Mr. Green.

Gus : *Yeah?*

Tillie goes on studying the hands of the players in the same casual way.

Gus chats on to her.

Gus : *See anybody else?*

Tillie is not worried.

Tielie : *Not a soul.*

The players stare each other out, then make their bids for new cards, which Gus deals.

Mr White : *I'll take three, Doctor.*

Mr Black off : *Five.*

Mr Green : *I'll have to play these, I guess.*

We are now back of Gus, as he turns up four aces and a deuce in his hand, palming up a card each time.

Gus off : *Uh-uh! Ahhh! My, my! Godfrey . . . Daniel . . . Charlie Boll and Doctor Bibi! Goodness gracious!* He raps the table. *Shucks!*

He wants more information.

Gus : *What happened to the two sailors?*

Tillie looks at Mr White's hand.

Tillie : *Three more sailors joined them.*

Gus is bemused.

Gus : *Three more sailors?*

Tllie is confused.

Tillie : *I mean two.*

Gus relaxes, ready to take the other three men.

Gus : *Oh, I thought so.*

The men put their money on the table.

Mr White : *I bet twenty-five dollars.*

MR BLACK: *I call it.*
MR GREEN: *I call.*
GUS: *I'm shy. I raise seventy-five.*
MR WHITE: *I call. I'm light, Doctor.*
MR GREEN: *I'll sell it. I'm light.*
MR BLACK: *I'll call, too.*
MR WHITE putting down his hand: *Four jacks.*
MR BLACK putting down his hand: *Four queens.*
MR GREEN putting down his hand: *I'm sorry, Doctor, it'll take four aces to beat me.*
GUS grinning: *What a coincidence . . .*
We see GUS's hand laying his cards on the table.
GUS off: *What a coincidence! Here they are!*
MR WHITE can't believe his eyes. Nor can MR BLACK. MR GREEN is green. TILLIE comes over to take the money as GUS scoops in the bills.
GUS: *May I remind you ecclesiastically that the pot was shy two hundred and twenty-five herring?*
TILLIE also gives her missionary blessing.
TILLIE: *You may keep it as a souvenir of a pleasant twenty minutes.*
Down the aisle, TILLIE and GUS walk in triumph.
GUS singing: *Bringing in the sheaves/Bringing in the she . . .*
Dissolve to a train seat, where GUS sits beside TILLIE, who is stuffing all the winnings in her bag.
GUS: *You're entitled to fifty per cent, my little Annie Oakley.*
TILLIE: *I shall credit your share to the alimony account.*

Fade out on GUS's look of disgust and fade into the living room of MARY's old home, where PHINEAS PRATT is explaining the will to the two missionaries, come back home for the share-out.
PRATT: *It was very sad, Tillie, but your brother died a bankrupt. Yes, sir, there just ain't no estate.*
Move back to show TILLIE and GUS.
TILLIE: *Instead of the pot of gold at the end of the rainbow, we found an ash can.*
GUS: *Tell me, Ash Can . . .*
PRATT: *Pratt! Phineas Pratt!*

93

TILLIE : *As children, we used to call him by another name.*

GUS : *And a very appropriate one, I'm sure.*

TILLIE : *What of the old home here? All these priceless heirlooms ought to fetch a tidy sum.*

PRATT : *No, it's all been sold, for the mortgage.*

GUS : *Who bought it?*

PRATT : *Er . . .* He laughs *. . . I did.*

GUS : *My sweet, loan me this handbag for a moment.*

He seems ready to brain PRATT, but TILLIE restrains him gently.

TILLIE : *What of this ferry boat you speak of?*

PRATT : *T'ain't worth nothin', but just to help Mary out, I offered her five hundred for it, but she refused.*

GUS sees something might be saved beside a soul.

GUS : *Refused five hundred? The poor girl must have been out of her mind with grief.*

PRATT sees an ally.

PRATT : *I wish you'd talk to Mary about it, for her own good.*

GUS and TILLIE rise to leave the frightful PHINEAS PRATT.

TILLIE : *We'll see what we can do.*

GUS : *Is this boat still above water?*

PRATT : *She still floats, but she can't run.*

Pan with the missionaries on their mission. GUS hits his cane on an antique vase, which rocks dangerously.

TLLIE : *Ugh . . .*

GUS : *Ahh! Just so.*

PRATT : *Careful! This is worth three thousand dollars.*

GUS : *Three thousand dollars . . .* He raps the vase *. . . for an overgrown shaving mug, and only five hundred dollars for a ferry boat?*

PRATT : *Well, I . . . I might pay Mary a little more. Yes, sir, just for . . . uh . . . . friendship.*

GUS : *Uh . . . how friendly? Say a thousand dollars?*

PRATT : *That's the limit.*

GUS : *At a thousand dollars, friendship ceases, eh?*

TILLIE : *You must be lonesome here with so many empty guest rooms.*

PRATT : *I'm never lonesome.*

He dismisses the heirs of the will.

PRATT : *Oh, by the way, if you're thinkin' of stayin' for a few days, the Commercial House is still the best hotel in town.*

A BUTLER comes in.

BUTLER : *Pardon, sir. Luncheon is served.*

PRATT : *You must excuse me, now.*

As he turns to go, we see TILLIE mouth curses at his back, which would be fine, only PRATT turns round again.

GUS : *I'll bet you haven't called him that since you were a child.*

Again GUS catches his cane on the vase. As it topples, he drops his cane and juggles the vase.

TILLIE : *Uhhh!*

PRATT is appalled with relief.

PRATT : *Uh . . . uh . . . uh . . .*

GUS : *A close shave*

TILLIE : *Augustus, your cane.*

She throws his cane to GUS who catches it and drops the vase with a crash.

GUS : *Come, my dear. Mind your footsies.*

Delicately, the missionaries pick their way out among the broken china.

Dissolve to a shot of a wharf, where there are workmen not working. GUS and TILLIE come onto the wharf and go over towards an old ferry-boat.

TILLIE : *Well, the Fairy Queen!*

GUS : *Looks more like an old Eskimo kyak.*

TILLIE : *Obviously the thing to do is to persuade my niece to take five hundred dollars for it.*

GUS : *You've been reading my mind.*

TILLIE : *Then we shall sell it to Phineas for a thousand, thus dividing five hundred dollars between us.*

GUS : *Not a bad day's work . . .* TILLIE laughs *. . . providing you don't do the dividing.*

Baby LeRoy, alias THE KING, stands on the edge of the boat. The anchor rope is round his waist to keep him from falling in. TILLIE and GUS view the look-out.

GUS : *What ho! The old ark is inhabited!*

THE KING looks down to see DOC the quacking goose in the water. He is joined by GUS and TILLIE.

GUS : *See here, young man, that is, if I'm not mistaken . . .*
From above, we see the tiny boy.
GUS off : *What is your name and where do you hail from?*
TILLIE shakes her head at GUS.
TILLIE : *Stupid! He can't understand you.*
GUS : *A foreigner, eh?*
As TILLIE laughs, GUS looks down to see the goose. Doc quacks.
GUS off : *Ah, a goose!*
GUS rises, pulling the goose on board by a string.
GUS : *A goose, if ever I saw one!*
TILLIE : *Do you like children?*
GUS : *I do if they're properly cooked.*
As TILLIE laughs, we see the little boy standing with the goose.
MARY comes forward to greet the newcomers.
MARY : *Excuse me.*
TILLIE : *Oh!*
MARY goes over to her little boy.
MARY : *King, what are you doing here?*
GUS : *I think he was going for a swim with the goose.*
MARY : *Isn't that just like a man! His father was supposed to watch him.*
GUS : *Who might his father be, Old Man River?*
MARY : *Well, you see, we . . . we live here.*
TILLIE : *You live here?*
MARY : *Yes. I . . . I own the boat.*
TILLIE turns on the charm.
TILLIE : *Child, doesn't your heart tell you? I'm your Aunt Tillie.*
GUS also simpers.
GUS : *And I am your Uncle Gussie.*
MARY and her KING are delighted.
MARY : *Uncle Gus and Aunt Tillie! Oh, I'm so happy. Well, when did you arrive?*
TILLIE off : *This morning.*
MARY : *We've been expecting you.* She calls. *Tom! Oh, Tom! My husband. You two are angels straight from heaven.*
This is a little much for GUS to swallow.
GUS : *Uh . . . we detoured slightly on the way.*
MARY holds her child and opens her heart.

96

MARY: *You're going to stay with us a long time, I hope. We can't offer you many luxuries, but we'll try to make you comfortable. Won't you come up to the living room while I fix some lunch?*

The prospect pleases GUS.

MARY: *I'll get Tom. He's probably in the engine room.*

MARY now puts KING in a high chair. He begins to whimper, while his mother hurries off.

MARY off: *It won't take a minute.*

TILLIE: *Sentimental little idiot, isn't she?*

GUS: *Yeah. Um-hmm.*

TILLIE: *It shouldn't be any trouble to persuade her to sell the boat for five hundred dollars.*

GUS: *She's a chump, if ever I saw one. Come, let's repair to the festive board.*

With a thud, he stubs his toe on the anchor.

KING gurgles with laughter. The anchor rope is still tied round his waist.

GUS looks at the offending piece of ironwork.

GUS: *Careless things, horses. Washington threw a dollar across the Potomac. I shall heave this horse anchor . . .*

TILLIE: *Augustus!*

GUS: *Don't annoy me.*

As he picks up the anchor to heave overboard, TILLIE stops him.

TILLIE: *The other end of that is attached to the baby!*

We see the rope on the laughing KING.

GUS off: *Trying to hold back on me, eh?*

TILLIE makes GUS drop the anchor. It hits his foot. GUS looks ready to explode as the baby gurgles with glee.

Dissolve to the dining-room of the ferryboat, with GUS and TILLIE, TOM and MARY and KING at table. GUS likes the look of the spread.

GUS: *Fodder fit for a king.*

As he grabs an ear of corn, TILLIE kicks him under the table. GUS hides the loot.

TOM is evidently as embarrassed as the missionaries on the subject.

TOM: *Uh . . . I suppose in your missionary work, it's customary to say grace.*

MARY : *Why, Tom, of course it is. Won't you say grace, Aunt Tillie?*

TILLIE : *Thank you, my dear, that's very thoughtful of you. I . . . However, I feel inadequate in the presence of your Uncle Augustus.*

GUS : *I shan't forget those words, my sweet. On the other hand, I'm a guest beneath this roof. The honor goes to the master of the house.*

TOM : *Well, I guess anybody can pray when they're happy.*

KING laughs at this.

TOM looks fondly at MARY.

TILLIE nudges GUS and both bow their heads.

MARY speaks the grace.

MARY : *We thank Thee for this meal and all Thy favours. We thank Thee also . . .*

TILLIE and GUS have to accept the blessing.

MARY off : *For the safe arrival of Aunt Tillie and Uncle Gus. May you guard them and protect them from harm. Amen.*

Under the table, DOC the goose eats the ear of corn that GUS is holding.

As TILLIE and the rest sit down to eat, GUS looks at the remains of his corn cob. He has to address the goose sternly.

GUS : *Would it be asking you too much to go away somewhere and lay an egg?*

The goose quacks right back.

Fade out and in to the engine room of the ferry-boat, where TOM is working away. MARY comes in.

MARY : *Where's Uncle Gus?*

TOM : *Oh, he decided to paint the boat.*

MARY : *Aunt Tillie insisted again on giving the baby his bath. The King loves her.*

TOM : *Oh, why not? You know I always figured missionaries would be something of . . . well, sort of depressing to have around the house. But Aunt Tillie and Uncle Gus are O.K.*

MARY : *It's been grand for us, having honest people to advise us.*

TOM : *I'll tell you something else grand. I'm liable to have this old engine running before the day is over.*

MARY : *You mean it?*

98

TOM: *Cross my heart.*

He crosses his heart, leaving a black smudge on his shirt, which MARY points out to him.

Inside a cabin on the boat, TILLIE is bathing the cooing KING.

TILLIE singing: *Throw out the life line/Throw out the life line/ Someone is drifting away . . . Give us the other hand. Come on, come on. Give us the pattie.*

Now we are closer on TILLIE and the baby.

TILLIE singing: *Throw out the life line/Throw out the life line/ Someone is sinking today . . . Now, come on.*

TILLIE's hands squeeze water over the baby's head.

TILLIE singing: *Someone is sinking today.*

The baby and TILLIE are in fits of laughter.

The baby pulls the plug out of the tub.

The water pours out, swamping everything.

TILLIE: *King!*

THE KING laughs up at TILLIE.

TILLIE: *Oh! Naughty!*

The baby just gurgles like the water.

Now we are on deck with GUS, trying to look nautical and fiddling with the radio's dial.

GUS: *Well, I'm on time today.*

VOICE off: *There should be a room in every house where the entire family can congregate and relax . . .*

SECOND VOICE off: *. . . The bathroom with its gleaming tiles . . .*

THIRD VOICE off: *. . . And now let me say a word about my lady's lingerie . . .*

FOURTH VOICE off: *It should be changed every thousand miles.*

As GUS fiddles with the dials, he consults a radio programme in a paper. At last, he finds the right voice, HANDY ANDY's.

ANDY off: *Hello, folks. Handy Andy speaking.*

GUS: *Ah!*

ANDY off: *Today I shall continue my subject, Mixing Paint for the Home.*

GUS checks out the cans and bottles and packages near him on the deck.

ANDY off: *You should have ready all the articles I mentioned yesterday.*

GUS: *Got 'em.*

ANDY off : *Are you ready?*

GUS : *Ready! Shoot!*

ANDY off : *Good! First take the turpentine can . . .* GUS takes the small can . . . *the large one.*

GUS : *Ah.*

He switches hastily to the large can of turpentine.

ANDY off : *Open a vent with an axe . . .*

GUS breaks the fire glass to get the axe out from behind it.

ANDY off : *Or a hatchet will do quite nicely.*

GUS : *Make up your mind.*

He swings the axe and only succeeds in denting the can.

GUS : *This is the way we used to open 'em in the army.*

He takes another swipe without making much more effect than a noise.

GUS : *Guess I was thinking of the navy.*

This time he cuts a hole in the can.

ANDY off : *Now take the can and pour the contents into a tub. And now the lamp black . . .*

Frantically GUS pours and grabs.

ANDY off : *The pound package, the drier and a pint can of shellac.*

GUS : *The drier and a pint of shellac.*

He looks around desperately for the items.

ANDY off : *Pour in the lamp black.*

GUS : *Pour in the lamp black.*

ANDY off : *Now the drier.*

GUS : *The drier.*

ANDY off : Throw in the can of shellac.

GUS throws in the tin can as well as the contents.

GUS : *Throw in the can of shellac.*

ANDY off : *Pay strict attention. Now stir rapidly with a paddle.*

GUS stirs the mixture as if winning a boat race.

ANDY off : *From now on we'll have to work faster to keep the mixture from coagulating.*

GUS gibbers as he stirs and grabs and measures and pours.

ANDY off : *Pour in the linseed oil . . .*

GUS : *Linseed oil.*

ANDY off : *Two cups of benzine . . .*

GUS : *Two cups of benzine.*

ANDY off : *Three scoops of white lead . . .*

GUS : *Three scoops . . .*
ANDY off : *The small can of turpentine, banana oil, and now the large bag of lamp black . . .*
GUS : *Large bag of lamp black. Large bag . . .*
ANDY off : *One capsule of Prussian blue . . .*
GUS : *One capsule of Prussian blue.*
ANDY off : *One scoop of the red tint . . .*
> GUS can't stand the pace.
GUS : *Not so fast, not so fast!*
ANDY off : *Stir slowly.*
> There is a moment of false relief.
ANDY off : *Two scoops white tint.*
GUS : *Two scoops . . .*
> HANDY ANDY is off to the races again.
ANDY off : *Stir quickly. Three scoops of flaked shellac. Stir lightly. Three dashes of alcohol. A pint of clarifier. One pint of drier. Two cups raw linseed oil.*
GUS : *You said that before!*
ANDY off : *Five pounds of grey.*
GUS : *Five pounds of grey.*
ANDY off : *Seven scoops of white lead.*
> GUS is frantic with trying to keep up.
ANDY off : *One package of yellow. One quart of thinner. Stir thoroughly.*
> Unseen to GUS, the baby totters in and changes the dial of the radio.
VOICE off : *Now, pay strict attention.*
> GUS drops the paint mixture over everything, as he follows the physical jerks.
VOICE off : *Up on your tiptoes. Take a deep breath. Exhale. Arms over the head. Raise the right knee. Now the left. The right. The left. The right. Left. Right. Left. Right. Left. Right . . . Rest.*
> GUS is covered with paint and sweat.
GUS : *Whew! here must be an easier way to mix paint!*
> Dissolve to the wharf where PHINEAS PRATT is with an official, COMMISSIONER MCLENNAN.
PRATT : *This is the boat, Commissioner.*
> He gives the COMMISSIONER the lowdown.
PRATT : *It should have been condemned years ago. He calls. Any-*

101

body aboard?

> MARY sees the pair on the wharf and leaves the boat to join them.

MARY: *Hello, Mr Pratt.*

PRATT: *Mrs Sheridan, this is Commissioner McLennan of the State Inspection Board.*

MARY: *How do you do? Won't you come in?*

McLENNAN: *No, thank you. I'm afraid I bring you rather unpleasant news.*

> TOM and TILLIE come in to join the group.

MARY: *Oh, Commissioner McLennan, this is my aunt, Mrs Winterbottom, and my husband.*

TOM: *How do you do?*

McLENNAN simultaneously: *How are you?*

TILLIE: *To what do we owe the honor of this visit?*

McLENNAN: *I have a paper for your signature, Mrs Sheridan.*

TOM: *What is it?*

McLENNAN: *A cancellation of your ferry franchise, to become effective July the fifth.*

MARY: *Our franchise cancelled? Tom!*

TOM: *Steady, honey!*

McLENNAN: *Now, if you'll just sign this, Mrs Sheridan.*

PRATT: *Here . . . here's a pen.*

> GUS comes on in the nick of time.

GUS: *Hold! Not so fast!*

> He moves close up to PRATT and McLENNAN.

TOM off: *Oh, Commissioner McLennan, this is my uncle, Mr Winterbottom.*

GUS: *Uh . . . did you write this?*

McLENNAN: *It's a legal form of cancellation.*

GUS: *No niece of mine shall ever sign it, by heck!*

> He tears up the paper.

PRATT: *But the old hulk ain't sea-worthy!*

GUS: *That's a downright fib.*

McLENNAN: *I'm not so sure. This boat was launched in 1881.*

GUS: *So was my wife, but she's still sea-worthy.*

> TILLIE doesn't like the sound of that at all.

McLENNAN: *She's probably got barnacles all over her.*

> He catches TILLIE's look of fury.

McLennan : *The boat, I mean!*

Gus : *She's as solid as a brick telephone booth.*

McLennan : *Well, I'll look it over.*

Gus : *Follow me.*

He takes McLennan off to the boat.

Tillie to Pratt : *I suppose if we dug deep enough we'd find you at the bottom of all this!*

Gus takes the Commissioner from a cabin onto the deck of the ship.

Gus : *The whole ship is put together like the Rock of Gibraltar.*

As he closes the cabin door, the knob comes off in his hand.

Gus : *My wife keeps this handy to darn my socks.*

The sign above the door clatters to the deck.

Gus : *This has no business here. It belongs in the front of my cap.*

McLennan : *It needs painting pretty badly.*

Gus : *Uh . . . uh . . . let me call your attention to these rails. Non-breakable and indestructible.*

As Gus pushes, the rail falls outwards, carrying Gus with it.

Gus hangs onto the rail for dear life.

Gus : *Detachable so we can handle the crowds!*

The life preserver falls off the rail down the boat's side.

In the water, the life preserver sinks like a millstone.

Gus looks down, then up again at McLennan.

Gus : *Lordie mercy!*

As Gus struggles back on deck to join the Commissioner, Pratt hurries in with Mary and Tom and Tillie. There is the sound of a boat's whistle, as all look off.

A new paddle-steamer is coming towards the dock.

On the paddle-wheel, its nostalgic name : 'KEYSTONE'. Back on the deck of the old 'FAIRY QUEEN', the commissioner congratulates Pratt.

McLennan : *Here comes your new boat, Phineas.*

Tillie : *I might have guessed it!*

Tom : *So you're cancelling our franchise and giving it to him!*

McLennan : *Not yet. However, with this boat out of commission, I . . .*

Tom : *By the Fourth of July, it'll be ready to operate again.*

Gus : *Practically as good as new.*

The engines of the new paddle-steamer sound nearby, a

warning that provokes a confrontation face to face.

PRATT: *Let 'em prove it!*

GUS: *What's your crooked proposition, Ash Can?*

PRATT: *A race between this boat and the new one.*

TILLIE: *A race!*

PRATT: *Yes, sir, from here to Old Town, and the first boat to reach the dock gets the franchise.*

McLENNAN: *How would the Fourth of July suit you as the day for the race?*

GUS: *Fourth of July? If it was good enough for Washington, it's good enough for me!*

The Commissioner turns to go.

McLENNAN: *Very well. Good day.*

GUS: *Uh . . .*

TILLIE: *Good day.*

McLENNAN: *Good day.*

PRATT: *Good day!*

PRATT follows the COMMISSIONER off the ship, as we pan to the crew of the 'FAIRY QUEEN'.

GUS: *Toodle-oodle. What are you kids laughing at?*

TILLIE: *I recall a dog-sled race in Canada some years ago. The slowest team won by forty minutes.*

GUS: *Uh . . . by some queer mischance, the runners of the fast sleigh got frozen in the ice.*

TILLIE: *Cheer up, my child. I'm sure that love . . . or your Uncle Augustus . . . will find a way.*

GUS: *I'll bend every effort to win this race, and I come from a long line of effort-benders.*

Fade out and in to the dock, where we see the name 'KEY-STONE' on the boat moored there.

Now we are underwater, where GUS is in a diving suit, blowing bubbles, his helmet sprouting tubes like Medusa.

Back on the dock, we start on the bow of the 'KEYSTONE', then we track to where TILLIE is pumping air down to the diver below. She speaks down another tube among a mess of diving gear.

TILLIE: *Gus, be sure you're under the right boat. Don't damage the Fairy Queen!*

The air pressure gauge looks rather low. There are some gurgling noises.

TILLIE speaks down the tube.

TILLIE: *Augustus!*

Underwater GUS is blowing bubbles and tying a rope to the support of the dock.

He ties the rope firmly as he gasps for air.

TILLIE off: *Augustus!*

On the dock, TILLIE stops pumping and speaks again.

TILLIE: *I'm tired of pumping air. Have you tied her to the dock yet?*

GUS's voice sounds hollow in the tube.

GUS off: *Not only that . . . I've disconnected, disturbed and otherwise unjointed her.*

TILLIE: *Good!*

TILLIE laughs, looks off, and sees—

CAPTAIN FOGG, skipper of the 'KEYSTONE', as he comes on his landlegs along the dock.

TILLIE throws a tarpaulin over the diving apparatus.

CAPTAIN FOGG lights his pipe, then moves on and comes up to TILLIE, just as she finishes getting everything concealed. She sits down.

CAPTAIN FOGG: *Good evening.*

TILLIE: *Good evening.*

The CAPTAIN sits down beside her. She glares at his pipe, which he puts aside.

CAPTAIN FOGG: *Do you know who I am?*

TILLIE: *No. Isn't there anyone around here who can tell you?*

CAPTAIN: *I'm the Captain of the Keystone.*

TILLIE: *Then what are you worrying about?*

Now we are close by a part of the diving gear with a sign: AIR INTAKE. Pan down to the pipe, pouring out tobacco smoke which is being sucked down the air vent.

Underwater, we are close on GUS with his diving helmet filling up with smoke.

GUS: *Hey!*

On the dockside, the uneasy TILLIE sits beside the gallant CAPTAIN.

GUS hollowly off: *Hey!*

105

TILLIE : *Mice!*

GUS off : *Air! More air!*

CAPTAIN FOGG ⎫
TILLIE ⎭   *What did you say?*

TILLIE : *I didn't say anything.*

CAPTAIN FOGG : *Well, somebody said something.*

GUS gasping off : *Air! Give me . . . give me ozone!*

TILLIE : *An echo.*

> She stuffs her handkerchief into the speaking tube.

CAPTAIN FOGG : *Echo of what?*

TILLIE : *Of what you said.*

CAPTAIN FOGG : *I said good evening.*

TILLIE : *Good night.*

CAPTAIN FOGG : *No, good evening.*

TILLIE : *I'm saying good night.*

> CAPTAIN FOGG knocks the ashes out of his pipe. The ashes
> fall into the vent.
>
> Underwater, GUS's helmet is full of smoke and ashes, as the
> diver gasps and gurgles.
>
> On the dock, CAPTAIN FOGG rises at last to go.

CAPTAIN FOGG : *Many strange things come out at night!*

> Underwater, GUS begins to pull himself to the surface by the
> lifeline. Bubbles burst out of his diving suit.
>
> By the dock, GUS comes out of the water in his diving suit
> like a spouting whale. He starts up the ladder.
>
> He opens up his diving helmet. Smoke pours out as he breathes
> again.

GUS : *Whew!*

> He loses his balance and pitches back off the ladder. He
> falls back into the sea, struggles about, then starts up the
> ladder again.
>
> Now he blows out water like a gargoyle gutter. He reaches
> the top of the ladder, where TILLIE is waiting alone. He takes
> off his diving helmet and manages to drop it on his foot. He
> is very pained.

GUS : Is there a doctor in the house?

> Fade out and in to a fireworks' explosion, then another cluster
> of rockets, as a band plays for the Fourth of July. Then dis-

solve to the river, where we see the 'KEYSTONE' and the 'FAIRY QUEEN' lined up side by side for the big race.

By the dockside, there are crowds of cheering people and a band playing.

On the bridge of the 'KEYSTONE', CAPTAIN FOGG reassures PHINEAS PRATT.

CAPTAIN FOGG: *That franchise is as good as in your pocket right now.*

PRATT: *I know that.*

They look down to see—

People milling about on the deck below.

Back on the bridge, PRATT objects and calls out.

PRATT: *Hey you! All of you . . .*

The people on deck look up at the sound of the voice.

PRATT off: *Keep off this boat!*

Beside his CAPTAIN, PRATT gives his reason.

PRATT: *We ain't goin' to carry no dead weight in this race. Take the Fairy Queen.*

On the deck of the 'KEYSTONE', the crowd begins to leave for the shore. On the dock itself, reporters and others crowd around GUS, who is holding onto THE KING.

REPORTER: *Will you make a statement about the race, and make it brief?*

GUS: *We can't lose.*

He goes off with the baby.

On the 'FAIRY QUEEN', TOM is agitated.

TOM: *Uncle Gus, come on! The race is gonna start in three minutes.*

On the dock, GUS does a deal with THE KING.

GUS: *Do me a favor, King, and don't require any service until this race is over.*

The baby just laughs at him.

As GUS and the baby lead the crowd towards the 'FAIRY QUEEN', a man comes on, wheeling a load of fireworks.

A lot of people crowd on board the 'FAIRY QUEEN' following GUS and the child. TOM and MARY try to stop them.

TOM: *Oh, hold on, folks, hold on! I'm sorry but you can't ride with us this trip.*

MARY: *Please, he means we can't win this race if we carry you all.*

107

And the race means our franchise.

A man called GRIDLEY steps forward to announce the race.

GRIDLEY: *I'm now ready to start this race. It will finish at the Old Town dock. The first boat to touch the slip wins.*

On the 'FAIRY QUEEN', the people begin to move off.

MARY: *Thanks a lot.*

TOM: *Oh, thanks. I knew you'd understand, all right.*

As the people go, they reveal the boxes of fireworks, somehow left on board.

TILLIE urges GUS to take command.

TILLIE: *Augustus, hurry up, get up there, take the wheel!*

GUS hands her the King.

GUS: *Take the baby, change a tire, get the plate off that door for the front of my cap.*

He leaves for the bridge.

GRIDLEY readies himself for action.

On the bridge of the 'KEYSTONE', CAPTAIN FOGG shouts his order with PRATT at his side.

CAPTAIN FOGG: *Stand by below!*

On the bridge of the 'FAIRY QUEEN', GUS takes hold of the wheel as TILLIE takes hold of THE KING.

TILLIE: *I suppose you couldn't win without that sign on your cap.*

GUS: *I could, but it wouldn't be official.*

GRIDLEY calls out from the crowd on the dock.

GRIDLEY: *Are you ready, Keystone?*

PRATT answers from his bridge.

PRATT: *Keystone ready.*

GRIDLEY calls out again from the dock.

GRIDLEY: *Ready, Fairy Queen?*

GUS pokes his head out of the window of the bridge of his ship.

GUS: *You may fire when ready, Gridley.*

GRIDLEY raises his starting gun and fires it. The band starts playing.

PRATT and CAPTAIN FOGG leap into action.

The paddle-wheel of the 'KEYSTONE' begins to churn. GUS pulls on the cord to signal the engine-room. It breaks in his hand, though the gong does sound.

GUS: *Busted!*

Now the paddle-wheel of the 'FAIRY QUEEN' begins to

turn and the boat begins to draw away.

The band plays and the people cheer as the old ferryboat moves off.

MARY comes on beside GUS.

GUS: *We're off! Come on.*

In the distance, we see the two boats, the 'FAIRY QUEEN' on its way, but the 'KEYSTONE' still tied to the dock.

MARY looks back and does not understand.

MARY: *What's the matter with the Keystone?*

GUS: *They'll find out.*

The paddle-wheels turn in the rival boat, but it is still tied to the dock.

PRATT and CAPTAIN FOGG are furious, as a sailor rushes on.

SAILOR: *Captain, we're tied to the dock with a rope.*

PRATT: *A rope! Cut it away!*

SAILOR: *Two men are cutting it away now, sir.*

In the engine-room of the 'FAIRY QUEEN', TOM is stoking the boilers furiously.

In the wheelhouse of the 'KEYSTONE', CAPTAIN FOGG is at the wheel as PRATT enters.

SAILOR off: *The rope is cut away, sir.*

CAPTAIN FOGG: *We're all right now.*

As the CAPTAIN spins the steering wheel, it falls off. Then it rolls across the deck of the 'KEYSTONE' and plunges into the water.

Back in the wheelhouse, there is panic.

CAPTAIN FOGG: *We're turning in a circle!*

PRATT: *Well, do something!*

CAPTAIN FOGG: *But the wheel's gone.*

PRATT: *The other wheelhouse!*

CAPTAIN FOGG: *Yeah, that's right.* He rushes off.

PRATT: *Ugh!*

He follows his CAPTAIN, mad with rage.

On the deck of the 'FAIRY QUEEN', GUS looks back.

GUS: *If my reckoning is right, the Keystone ought to turn over any minute now.*

On the 'KEYSTONE', PRATT and CAPTAIN FOGG go into the upper wheelhouse.

Now we see the 'KEYSTONE' from far away.

117

Ahead of it, its rival ferry, the 'FAIRY QUEEN'.

Inside his engine-room, TOM feeds the fires.

Inside the wheelhouse, GUS is at the wheel, with MARY and TILLIE nearby, and THE KING pulling on the whistle-cord of the boat.

TOM is looking worried in the engine-room.

The pressure gauge goes down to 20, as steam escapes from the whistle.

TOM hears the whistle and yells up.

Inside the wheelhouse, GUS hears TOM's voice.

TOM off: *Gus! Gus!*

At that moment, THE KING lets the whistle-cord drop.

GUS: *Hello! Hello, below!*

TOM is yelling down in the engine-room.

TOM: *Stop it! Stop it!*

In the wheelhouse, GUS is listening.

GUS: *Stop what? The boat?*

TOM explains.

TOM: *No, the whistle.*

TILLIE hands the baby over to GUS.

TILLIE: *Here, Gus, get him out of here before we lose this race.*

MARY: *I'll take the wheel.*

GUS comes on deck with THE KING. He points out a pretty sight.

Well behind, the 'KEYSTONE' tries to catch up.

GUS looks to the baby for approval.

GUS: *There she lies, King, wallowing in our wake.*

In the wheelhouse of the 'KEYSTONE', PRATT and CAPTAIN FOGG use every ounce of effort and will in hot pursuit.

On the deck of the 'FAIRY QUEEN', GUS takes a poll.

GUS: *King, what is your honest opinion of Phineas Pratt?*

THE KING blows a raspberry.

Inside his engine-room, TOM is running short on fuel.

TOM: *Hey, Gus! Wood! More wood!*

He runs out up the iron ladder.

He rushes onto the deck.

TOM: *Gus! Gus, I'm running out of firewood. Get some more quick!*

GUS off: *Coming, Tommy.*

Tom goes back down.

Gus takes his leave of The King.

Gus : *Duty calls, King, all hands below.*

Another long shot of the two ferry-boats shows them quite close together now.

In the wheelhouse of the 'KEYSTONE', Pratt listens to his Captain.

Captain Fogg : *Well, we're gaining on 'em.*

Seen from above the deck of the 'FAIRY QUEEN', Gus comes on with the baby. Pan with him as he puts the child in a small tub and leaves. He then gets a rope tied onto a bucket and ties it onto the tub. The little boy gurgles and whistles with glee.

Now Gus unties another rope round a stack of wood on the deck. He picks up one log and carries it off. The other logs roll down the deck and off the ship.

The King gurgles as the wood falls off the ship.

Gus chucks his log down the chute to the engine-room.

Gus : *Look out below, and there's plenty more where this came from.*

As he speaks, he looks back to see . . .

The logs all floating away.

Gus chides the dumb bits of wood.

Gus : *That's gratitude for you, leaving their own fireside.*

Tom off : *Hey, Gus, wood! More wood!*

Gus : *O.K.*

He starts out to look for timber.

The 'KEYSTONE' draws nearer and nearer to the 'FAIRY QUEEN'.

On the deck of the 'FAIRY QUEEN', Gus finds an axe and starts to chop through a supporting beam.

Gus : *Ah, a cherry tree!*

The head of the axe smashes into the lifeboat, holing it in one.

Gus slips and kicks the bucket that is tied to the baby's tub.

Gus : *The breaks are against me!*

The bucket falls over the side of the ferry-boat into the water. Pan with The King as the tub and baby begin to slide down the deck, pulled by the rope on the bucket overboard.

119

Gus chucks anything wooden down the chute, including the broom.

In the engine-room, Tom stokes the fire with bits and pieces and old rope.

The 'KEYSTONE' gains steadily on the 'FAIRY QUEEN'.

In his wheelhouse, Pratt exults to Captain Fogg.

Pratt : *Well, we caught up to her!*

On the deck of the 'FAIRY QUEEN', Gus wheels up the boxes of fireworks.

The bucket over the side begins to sink, pulling down the rope tied to the tub.

The gurgling baby is dragged in the tub to the edge of the deck.

The bucket sinks.

The baby in the tub teeters on the brink.

King : *Mama! Mama!*

Doc the goose is on watch.

The baby falls over the side of the boat in the tub.

The goose quacks an alarm.

The tub floats away with the baby inside.

The goose walks off, quacking.

Gus throws the boxes of fireworks down the chute to the engine-room.

The goose comes quacking into the wheelhouse, where Mary and Tillie are at the wheel.

Tillie : *Shoo!*

The goose goes on quacking the alarm and pecking at Tillie who is trying to steer.

Tillie : *Shoo! Shoo! Stop it!*

The goose moves off, directing Tillie's gaze to see—

The baby in the tub, floating far away.

Tillie hands over to Mary.

Tillie : *Mary! The King! He's overboard! Now, now, now, you go to the wheel. Go to the wheel, my dear. I'll have Gus lower a lifeboat. Don't you worry.*

She runs off and shouts down to Gus.

Tillie : *Gus! Oh, Gus!*

Gus looks up from the deck.

Tillie points off.

TILLIE: *The King! He's overboard!*
>Gus cannot believe her, until he looks to see—
>The baby floating in the tub.
>Gus rushes off and gets into the lifeboat. We see him from above as he lowers the lifeboat from inside it by dropping its nose into the drink.
>He loosens the ropes and starts off.
>Pan with him on the rescue.
>But Gus has axed a hole in the lifeboat. He goes down with the water flooding all round him.

GUS: *Goodness gracious! The river is rising!*
>At this, the lifeboat capsizes.
>Gus swims about hopefully, his cigar still between his teeth.

GUS: *Throw out the lifeline! Throw out the lifeline!*
>TILLIE rushes onto the deck and begins to untie the life-raft.
>The raft breaks loose and falls overboard, taking TILLIE with it.
>TILLIE swims towards the raft. So does GUS.
>TILLIE urges him on, as she reaches the raft.

TILLIE: *Gus, come on! Hurry!*
>Gus and TILLIE reach the raft, and he clambers on. While she gets on, he wrings out the water from his cigar, then begins to paddle with his cane.

TILLIE: *Hurry, Gus, hurry!*

GUS: *Fear not, my little waterlily!*
>They both start paddling to the rescue. In the wheelhouse of the 'KEYSTONE', the villains exult.

CAPTAIN FOGG: *They're all overboard!*

PRATT: *I hope they drown!*
>Gus and TILLIE paddle valiantly in the raft.

GUS: *Hold everything, King, the Navy is coming.*
>The baby gurgles happily in his tub, then reaches down and pulls the plug out.
>TILLIE looks appalled to see—
>The baby playing with the plug.
>She warns GUS.

TILLIE: *Good heavens, look!*
>The baby drops the plug as the water begins rising in the sinking tub.

TILLIE and GUS paddle madly and reach the tub, just as it sinks.

GUS : *Come here, Captain Kidd.*

GUS gets the cooing baby aboard the raft.

GUS : *Once aboard the lugger, you'll be O.K.*

TILLIE : *Is he all right?*

GUS : *He's a little wet, but he's used to that.*

TILLIE : *Give him to me.*

In the wheelhouse of the 'FAIRY QUEEN', MARY is radiant.

MARY : *Thank heaven he's safe!*

On the raft, TILLIE congratulates her old man.

TILLIE : *Gus, you saved the King!*

GUS : *Long live the King, but look at the Queen!*

The 'KEYSTONE' is pulling level with the 'FAIRY QUEEN'.

On the wharf of the Old Town, which is the finishing line, a crowd waits with some cameramen. One of the cameramen walks backwards and falls into the water.

In the wheelhouse of the 'KEYSTONE', CAPTAIN FOGG and PRATT see victory in their grasp.

PRATT : *Full speed ahead!*

In the engine-room of the 'FAIRY QUEEN', TOM stokes the fires with the boxes of fireworks.

Explosions and stars shoot out of the smokestack of the 'FAIRY QUEEN'.

Rockets bombard the 'KEYSTONE', shot from the stack of its rival.

Fireworks explode in the wheelhouse of the 'KEYSTONE', making CAPTAIN FOGG and PRATT jump.

PRATT : *Oh! Oh! Lookit!*

PRATT catches ablaze.

PRATT : *Oh! I'm on fire! Oh! Oh! Oh!*

He leaps onto the deck, smoking and pursued by bangs.

A firecracker goes off in his trousers.

PRATT : *Ohhh!*

He jumps overboard to put himself out.

CAPTAIN FOGG is also on fire.

CAPTAIN FOGG : *Roman candles! Pinwheels! Sky rockets! Gosh!*

In the engine-room of the 'FAIRY QUEEN', TOM adds

boxes of fireworks to the barrage.

More explosions and rockets spout from the 'FAIRY QUEEN' at its rival.

Down in the engine-room, TOM piles more fireworks on the blaze. The boat starts to shake. As TOM runs for it up the ladder, the whole furnace and boiler explodes.

The explosion shoots the 'FAIRY QUEEN' ahead of the 'KEYSTONE', as if it were rocket-propelled.

From the deck of the 'FAIRY QUEEN, we see the wharf nearing and the people cheering.

The prow of the 'FAIRY QUEEN' smashes into the dock.

MARY and TOM fall into each others' arms in the wheelhouse.

MARY: *What happened?*

TOM: *Oh, we've won, darling, we've won!*

MARY: *Oh!*

On the raft, GUS and TILLIE and KING paddle in.

TILLIE: *Gus, we won! We won!*

GUS begins to whistle: 'Yankee Doodle Dandy'.

PRATT swims towards the raft and hangs onto the side.

PRATT: *Help!*

GUS looks down at the wet PHINEAS.

GUS: *I've been often told that rats couldn't swim.*

As PRATT moans and sinks under, GUS saves him by hooking his cane round the villain's neck and treading on it. On the wharf, the people are all over TOM and MARY.

MAN: *Good Work, Tom! I knew you could win!*

SECOND MAN: *Gee, what a race!*

WOMAN: *Atta-girl, Mary!*

MAN: *Hurray for the Fairy Queen!*

MARY: *There they are!*

TOM: *Oh, the King!*

They push their way off to see . . .

GUS and TILLIE and the baby paddling towards the wharf with the half-drowned PRATT clinging on for dear life.

TOM *leans down and takes the baby boy. Pan up with* TILLIE *as she gets onto the wharf.*

GUS has PRATT on his cane, hooked, lined up and sinking.

GUS: *Ash Can, you're a crook, and we have the papers to prove it.*

PRATT: *No!*

Gus ducks Pratt's head below the water.

Tom and Mary and the crowd look down at this rough justice. The King laughs with glee. Gus pulls the gasping Pratt up to the surface.

Gus : *Now! The new ferry-boat and the franchise both belong to Mary.*

Pratt has had enough of the water.

Pratt : *Yes. I took her money.*

Gus : *That's all we want to know.*

The Sheriff has heard this confession from the wharf. He comes down and takes the dripping Pratt off to jail.

Dissolve to the living-room of Mary's old family house, where Gus is now crawling on the floor with Doc the goose on his back, just to amuse the laughing King, Tom, Mary and Tillie.

Gus : *Choo-choo.* Laughter. *Choo-choo.* More laughter.

Tillie sees who has won the race twice over.

Tillie : *The Fairy Queen wins!*

All : *Hurray! Hurray!*

The Butler comes in to announce the meal.

Butler : *Mrs Sheridan. Dinner is served.*

Before they go off to eat, the master of the house has his say.

Tom : *I claim that ferry-boat race was the world's greatest gamble.*

Gus : *No. Don't forget Lady Godiva put everything she had on a horse.* He bursts into song. *Bringing in the sheaves . . .* Tillie laughs. *Bringing in the sheaves . . .*

All singing : *We will come rejoicing/Bringing in the sheaves.*

THE BANK DICK

A NOTE ON THIS EDITION

The version of *The Bank Dick* printed in this edition is that of the original screenplay; all major differences between this version and the final film are described in the notes to the screenplay.

Our thanks are due to Universal City Studios, Inc., for supplying a copy of the original screenplay for the preparation of this volume, and to Columbia Pictures Corporation, Ltd., for providing a print of *The Bank Dick*.

CREDITS:

Directed by	Edward Cline
Production company	Universal
Original story and screenplay by	Mahatma Kane Jeeves (W. C. Fields)
Photography	Milton Krasner
Art direction	Jack Otterson
Film editor	Arthur Hilton
Musical director	Charles Previn
Running time	74 minutes
First shown	1940

CAST:

Egbert Sousé	W. C. Fields
Agatha Sousé	Cora Witherspoon
Myrtle Sousé	Una Merkel
Elsie Mae Adele Brunch Sousé	Evelyn Del Rio
Mrs Hermisillo Brunch	Jessie Ralph
J. Pinkerton Snoopington (Johnson)	Franklin Pangborn
Joe Guelpe	Shemp Howard
Mackley Q. Greene (Dodds)	Richard Purcell
Og Oggilby	Grady Sutton
J. Frothingham Waterbury	Russell Hicks
Mr Skinner	Pierre Watkin
Filthy McNasty (a crook)	Al Hill
Cozy Cochran (a crook)	George Moran
Otis	Bill Wolfe
A. Pismo Clam	Jack Norton
Assistant Director	Pat West
Francois	Reed Hadley
Miss Plupp	Heather Wilde
Doctor Stall	Harlan Briggs
Mr Cheek	Bill Alston

126

A paper dragon about fifteen feet long and looking like the real McCoy scuttles along the ground. It comes to a sign which reads: "Lake Talahasee". The dragon moves on to take in a small shed like a piano-box. The flap of the shed is up to disclose an ice-box. A sign is in evidence:

EGBERT SOUSE
Fish for Sale
Condolences Free

We now see that the fake monster is being pulled on a rope by an obnoxious-looking moppet. He is making a sound which he fondly hopes is that of a reptile on the loose. With him is a small friend, a realist, who eyes him scornfully, as he says:

SECOND BOY: *Come on — let me pull him.*

FIRST BOY shaking his head and jeering: *If you had the rope, nobody'd know which end the dragon was on!*

The SECOND BOY is filled with righteous anger. He snarls, not very originally.

SECOND BOY: *Is that so?*

And forthwith biffs his selfish companion. The FIRST BOY lets out a howl of pain, drops the rope, and a fight begins. As they scuffle, a gust of wind lifts the dragon onto the lake beside which the incident has occurred. We follow the fearsome spectre as it starts on its way, then rapidly look past it, farther out on the lake, to pick up a strange and mellifluous character.

EGBERT SOUSE, a scholar, gentleman and judge of good grape, is sitting in a small rowboat. He has a fishing pole in his hand and is engrossed in conversation with a raven, one NICODEMUS, who is perched on the gunwhale. The sound of the boys' fight comes over, distantly.

EGBERT: *Life, my ebony friend, is a simple proposition.*

He scowls off at the interruption given his thought by the shore noises and says, without raising his voice:

127

EGBERT: *Quiet, please. You'll scare the fish.* Continuing to NICO-
DEMUS: *As I said, life is . . .*
NICODEMUS unexpectedly: *What fish, Egbert?*
EGBERT: *Ah, the realistic touch! You know there are no fish in
this lake — and I know it. But fortunately the suckers aren't as
wise as we are.*
NICODEMUS: *They never are.*

> EGBERT gives a snort and pulls in his line. As he does so, we
> see that it is baited with a jug. His mood lightens perceptibly
> as he uncorks the jug, saying:

EGBERT: *Yes, life is a simple affair — full of simple pleasures such
as a beneficient draught of nectar cooled in the depths of a fishless
lake.*

> He's about to take a slug, when his eye catches on something
> off. As his gazes fixes . . .
> The DRAGON is blowing across the lake and looking for all the
> world like a sea serpent.
> EGBERT jumps, so that his rugged, Western hat is almost dis-
> located from his shapely skull.
> The DRAGON is skittering along fearsomely.
> EGBERT is profoundly moved by the demonstration.

EGBERT: *Perhaps life isn't so simple after all, Nicodemus. A sea
serpent in a fishless lake!*

> He is about to take another drink when NICODEMUS croaks
> sternly:

NICODEMUS: *Quoth the raven — nevermore!*

> EGBERT looks at him, and then the jug. He nods guiltily.

EGBERT: *I see what you mean.*

> Sadly he tosses the jug overboard, just as there is a call off:

VOICE: *Egbert — Egbert Souse!*
EGBERT: *Sousé, please — accent grave over the "e".*
VOICE: *Egbert — come here!*

> EGBERT obviously is willing to oblige. He quickly picks up
> the oars and calls:

EGBERT: *Coming, friend.*

> He looks in the direction of the DRAGON, and adds to NICO-
> DEMUS:

EGBERT: *And gladly!*

> A disgruntled fisherman is standing on a small float when

EGBERT pulls up. He has a great deal of fishing gear but no fish. EGBERT knows this but as he clambers cheerfully out of his boat he says:

EGBERT: *Greetings, Mr Harris — and how went the piscatory adventure?*

HARRIS gloomily: *Didn't catch a thing — just like last year.*

EGBERT: *Then maybe you'd like a little help, like last year?*

HARRIS: *Yeah — I guess so.*

EGBERT goes to the shed, his place of business, near the float. At the shed, EGBERT opens the ice-box as he chants:

EGBERT: *Always ready to help out the unfortunate, yes indeed. Why go home empty-handed to face the mocking jeers of the family circle? Now here is a tasty sea bass — a splendid specimen of young fishhood.*

HARRIS annoyed: *How can I say I caught a sea bass here?*

EGBERT: *Would you believe that just now I almost caught a sea serpent?*

HARRIS: *No.*

EGBERT: *No, I guess not. But I did. Yes sir, had him hooked — fierce battle and all — but he got away.*

As he speaks he starts to wrap up the fish but HARRIS stops him.

HARRIS: *Haven't you any trout?*

EGBERT shaking his head: *Several other gentlemen also had a lamentable lack of luck this morning. All sold out except this.*

He holds up the sea bass again, but Harris waves it away.

HARRIS: *I got an idea the only fish around here are in your ice-box.*

As he starts away, EGBERT looks after him disappointedly.

EGBERT: *What a lack of faith!*

There is a raucous laugh off. He turns in the other direction. NICODEMUS is sitting on the Lake Talahasee sign.

NICODEMUS: *You better get a new racket, my son, my son.*

EGBERT enters to him, sea bass in hand.

EGBERT: *Suckers forget, my midnight magpie! Next season they'll be back to try again . . . Meanwhile, I shall repair to the bosom of my family — a dismal place I admit — and with this tasty token . . .*

He holds up the sea bass, and finishes with a sudden firmness.

EGBERT continuing : *I shall clout the first member of the tribe who contends — as is usual upon my return — that I am a loafer, ne'er-do-well, and double-gaited soldier of misfortune!*

As he starts away, the raven croaks :

NICODEMUS : *Hear! Hear!*

EGBERT halts, then decides to let it pass. He is before the fish house. He lets down the flap. On it is painted :

Closed for the Season

As he does this he addresses the fish in his hand.

EGBERT : *Let us not heed such jibes, my fine finny friend. For tomorrow morning, in my own little house, you and I will be having breakfast together!*

As he speaks, we see a close shot of the fish.

Dissolve to the same fish, which is now only an outline in bones, on a platter. Camera pulls back to reveal it is on a breakfast table.[1]

We are inside the modest home of the EGBERT SOUSE's in Lompoc, Kansas. Seated at the table are MRS AGATHA SOUSE, her mother, MRS HERMISILLO BRUNCH, and little ELSIE MAE ADELE BRUNCH SOUSE. MRS BRUNCH is an old nag and a scold. While the women talk, they continue to eat. Obviously they have knocked off EGBERT's sea bass.

A slight noise is heard overhead.

MRS BRUNCH : *What's he up to now — what's he up to?*

MRS SOUSE : *Your guess is as good as mine, Mother. I never know what to expect next.*

MRS BRUNCH : *Well, I bet anything he's been smoking again up in his room. This time, Agatha, you've just got to tell him to stop. If he doesn't I'm going back to my mother!*

ELSIE MAE : *You can't — grandpa's already there.*[2]

MRS BRUNCH : *Coming home from a whole summer's fishing — with one fish. Imagine!*

She picks vindictively at the remaining bones and continues.

MRS BRUNCH : *What does he think we're going to live on this winter — fish bones?*

MRS SOUSE with a sigh : *I suppose he'll try and support us like he did last year.*

MRS BRUNCH: *Imagine a man trying to take care of his family by attending theatre bank nights, working puzzle contests and suggesting slogans!*

MRS BRUNCH takes more toast and peanut butter and continues:

MRS BRUNCH: *He fairly reeks of smoke and liquor — if it ain't that, it's sen-sen.*

MRS BRUNCH returns the peanut butter to AGATHA. The telephone bell rings. As ELSIE MAE starts to make an impulsive dash for it, MRS SOUSE stops her.

MRS SOUSE: *Don't answer it, Elsie Mae. It's probably the LaCavas wanting their lawn mower back, and we're not finished with it yet.*[3]

From out of his bedroom EGBERT emerges. He is carrying what looks to be an ashtray, full of butts. Even now he is smoking one of the forbidden cigarettes. The sound of the ringing telephone comes over — as well as MRS BRUNCH's unpleasant voice.

MRS BRUNCH: *Ringing telephones, and the house smelling of smoke all the time — I tell you Agatha, I can't stand it much longer.*

As he hears this, EGBERT looks at the receptacle in his hand. Then he reaches up and screws it onto the chandelier, and we understand why the house smells of smoke.

EGBERT looks very pleased with himself. He doubles the lighted end of his cigarette back into his mouth with the well-known trick of the tongue and lips, and starts downstairs.[4]

He cannot talk now, of course.[5] EGBERT sees ELSIE MAE has his favourite detective story magazine. He tries to snatch it from her hand. ELSIE MAE jumps up from chair and kicks EGBERT on the shins. Smoke pours from both EGBERT's nostrils. He spits out the cigarette with a groan.

MRS SOUSE: *Mother was right. You have been pilfering a smoke in your room!*

EGBERT looks at the table — indicates the platter.

EGBERT: *Yeah — while you've been committing grand larceny on my sea bass!*

MRS BRUNCH: *There you go — begrudging us every mouthful we eat.*

EGBERT: *Fairest of mother-in-laws, if I begrudged every time you filled that mammoth cave of yours . . .*

131

Dreamily, he goes into a reverie.

EGBERT continuing: *Ah — mammoth cave. How well I remember when I was a guide in the Mammoth Cave in Kentucky. With knapsack and alpenstock I trudged along . . .*

He looks speculatively at his mother-in-law.

EGBERT continuing: *Open your mouth.*

Fascinated, she obeys. He shakes his head.

EGBERT continuing: *Wrong cave . . . Where's Myrtle?*

MRS SOUSE: *She's out waving to Og Oggilby.*

EGBERT: *And what is Og Oggilby — a parade?*

MRS BRUNCH: *He's a nice young man who works in the bank — and you keep away from him.*

ELSIE MAE: *Yeah — Sis' has almost got the jerk hooked.*

EGBERT: *What a romantic age this turns out to be! The jerk hooked! Which reminds me that you sea bass bandits have made it necessary for me to repair to the Black Pussy Cat Grill.*[6]

As he starts past ELSIE MAE, he grabs again for the magazine, this time successfully. Once more ELSIE MAE kicks his shins. This time he hits ELSIE MAE on the head with his knuckles a resounding clunk and walks hurriedly toward the door.

ELSIE MAE reaches for catsup bottle, throwing it at EGBERT. As EGBERT reaches for his hat, the catsup bottle strikes him on the back of the head. With a groan, EGBERT goes out of the door.

As EGBERT comes out of the front door he sees his daughter, MYRTLE, hanging over the front gate talking to a moon-faced young man. This spectacle of young love inspires EGBERT and he comes gaily to them, willing to help things.[7]

EGBERT: *Greetings, Myrtle, my bud — greetings and a busk.*

He kisses her lightly on the cheek, adding:

EGBERT continuing: *Do I intrude?*

MYRTLE: *Father — this is Og Oggilby, he . . .*

EGBERT: *Say no more! I can see from the light that shines like a beacon from his steadfast eyes (the good one), that his intentions are honorable. And I approve — most heartily I approve. You work in a bank and I love banks. Young man, you have my blessing.*

OG: *I — er —*

EGBERT raising his hand: *Tut — tut. Let us have no false modesty, pray. I am for you, pal . . .*

He slaps OG so heartily on the back he almost knocks him over.

EGBERT *continuing* : . . . *a hundred and six percent!*

MYRTLE *nervously* : *My father has been away!*

From the way she says the last word it is apparent what her thoughts are. EGBERT gets it — although a little surprised.

EGBERT : *Oh, sharper than a serpent's tooth . . . Well, nice to have met you, Og — and I hope the percentage works both ways . . . Good morning.*

He lifts his hat politely. As he passes MYRTLE he murmurs.

EGBERT : *Has he any moolah?*

Continuing on, he leaves OG and MYRTLE. OG looks after him fascinated and startled.[8]

OG : *Gee!*

EGBERT is approaching an unusual and easily recognizable car parked at the curb. Its hood is up and the CHAUFFEUR is working on the engine. EGBERT walks up and sticks his head into the car's works. He taps the CHAUFFEUR on the shoulder.

EGBERT : *What seems to be the trouble?*

The CHAUFFEUR ignores him.

EGBERT : *How's your compensator? How's the armature working? It might be the points. Have you had the brakes tested lately?*[9]

CHAUFFEUR *under his breath* : *Scram.*

The LADY *in the car now sticks her head out of the window.*[10]

LADY : *Listen to the gentleman attentively, James — be polite.*

EGBERT lifts his hat to the LADY, asks James :

EGBERT : *Have you a shifting spanner?*

CHAUFFEUR : *A what?*

EGBERT : *A monkey wrench.*

LADY *as James hesitates* : *Get the gentleman what he asks for, James.*

James obeys reluctantly. He throws EGBERT the spanner.[11] EGBERT starts screwing a bolt under the engine, talking as he does so.

EGBERT : *This is all you need to do . . . just screw this thing up here . . . and . . .*

He gives the bolt a vicious turn and the front of the engine falls out of the car. EGBERT straightens up, hands the spanner

133

to CHAUFFEUR.

EGBERT: . . . *Well, get that back up there and maybe tighten it up a little more — I'll stop on my way back.*

LADY interrupting: *Thank you, sir.*

The CHAUFFEUR glares. EGBERT doffs his hat politely and walks on down the street.

The cafe is on the corner of the main street and lane leading from it. Near it, set back from the curbing, is a bench. A sign reads: BUS STOP. EGBERT arrives in front of the cafe, tries the door. It is locked. EGBERT looks at sign painted on the door.

INSERT:

BLACK PUSSY CAT GRILL
The Best Food and Beverage in Town

Tacked beside it is a small, written sign which says:

Out to Breakfast
Joe

EGBERT has finished looking at sign. He moves toward bench at bus stop. He arrives at bench. A GIRL is sitting there. She is reading a book. EGBERT tips his hat, ingratiatingly.

EGBERT: *May I share this seat with you?*

GIRL without looking up from book: *It's bus property.*

EGBERT: *Oh yes, so it is . . .* he sits . . . *Lovely weather we're having.*

GIRL coldly: *It was.*

EGBERT: *So it was — so it was.*

GIRL continues reading her book. EGBERT takes a newspaper from his pocket which he starts to read noisily. While he is going through this newspaper routine, an open roadster drives up.

The car stops at the bench. A nicely dressed young man is driving it. The GIRL looks up and smiles coyly.

GIRL as car stops beside her: *Oh, hello there . . .*

The young man turns and looks at GIRL. It is evident that he does not know her, but still he opens the door of the car.

GIRL rises, places book on bench, gets into car. They drive off.

134

EGBERT, who has seen the situation, looks down, picks up book the GIRL has left, turns it over and looks at title.

INSERT:

HOW TO WIN FRIENDS AND
INFLUENCE PEOPLE

EGBERT: *She must have read the last chapter first.*
EGBERT places book alongside of him, is about to continue reading paper, then looks up.

JOE, the bartender, is unlocking the door of the Black Pussy Cat.
EGBERT rises hurriedly. JOE is just about to enter when EGBERT comes to him.

EGBERT with a raffish leer: *The best food and beverage in town, eh?*

JOE unlocking door imperturbably: *That's what the sign says.*
They enter the café.

Inside the café: the bar on the side, some tables, booths on the other side, and in the rear — a service opening from the kitchen. JOE and EGBERT enter. JOE ducks under the bar.

JOE: *What's your pleasure?*

EGBERT: *Fishing — but right now I want a poultice.*
JOE turns to prepare the drink. OTIS enters.

EGBERT: *Hello, Otis.*

OTIS: *How are you, Mr Souse?*

EGBERT: *Soo-zay — accent grave over the " e ".*

OTIS to JOE: *Gimme a beer.*
JOE hands EGBERT his poultice, and as he is drawing the beer . . .

OTIS: *See there's a moving picture company from Hollywood working down near your house.*

EGBERT sipping his drink: *I noticed some unseemly disturbance on my way here. But I put it down to general unsettled conditions. Movies, eh? Did you know that I once was identified with the cinema — and vice versa? Willie the Conqueror, they called me.*

As he has been speaking, OTIS sips at his beer, paying small heed. Now he sets the glass down, and seeing a fly on the bar

135

is about to make a swipe at it with his hand when he is stopped by EGBERT.

EGBERT : *Don't hurt that fly — that's Old Tom — they named a gin after him. That fly followed me out here from the show.*

OTIS : *What show?*

EGBERT : *Don't interrupt. He used to drive in the chariot races in the flea circus.*

OTIS to JOE : *Gimme a cigar.*

JOE moves toward bar to get it.

EGBERT : *One afternoon in a small town outside of Hoosic Falls, when I was ignominiously dragged off to the local bastille and placed in durance vile at the behest of a blackguard regarding the loss of his silver timepiece . . .*

OTIS : *Well, did he say you stole his watch?*

EGBERT : *Hold your thought, Otis . . . Old Tom, feeling he was implicated — remembering the adage — " Time Flies " . . .*

JOE is handing the open cigar box to OTIS. As OTIS is taking a cigar from the box :

OTIS : *I was goin' to say . . .*

EGBERT : *I'll have a cigar. Thanks . . . twenty-five cents . . . thanks . . .*

JOE offers box to EGBERT. EGBERT takes one. OTIS looks on in amazement. Places money on bar.

OTIS placing money on bar : *I don't want to hear any more about it.*

EGBERT slapping his upper coat pocket, paying absolutely no attention : *I'll smoke it after Tiffin . . . to continue, my friend, Old Tom, the fly, stuck his left hind leg into the Governor's inkwell, dragged it above the dotted line, forging the Governor's signature. The Governor's secretary, unaware of the hoax, inadvertently picked up the document, gave it to a messenger and sent it to the warden who released me with profuse apologies. I love that fly.*

OTIS : *I don't care what he done, I'll kill him if he gets in my ear again.*

During this speech an agitated newcomer has entered the saloon. He goes to the phone by the bar and dials quickly. EGBERT is giving OTIS the evil eye, and is just finishing as he asks for party.[12]

EGBERT to OTIS : *It's men like you that give this town a bad name.*

136

You make me shudder — you killer.

The newcomer, MARTIN DODDS,[13] now has his party and his excited voice comes over:

DODDS: *But I tell you he's drunk, J.R.*[14]

EGBERT turns immediately to listen.

DODDS continuing into the telephone: *... said he had trouble with his wife ... Yes. We have tried, but he isn't sober! The best I can? But J.R., you don't understand! Hello ... hello ...*

He realizes that the boss has hung up. He replaces the receiver, muttering:

DODDS continuing: *Do the best I can!*

He goes over to where EGBERT is standing at the bar.

DODDS: *Give me whatever you've got for the jitters.*

EGBERT helpfully: *Joe, if the gentleman has butterflies in the stomach, I suggest a Suisses with a dash of dog in it.*

DODDS: *Dog?*

EGBERT: *Absinthe.*

The newcomer nods assent; obviously he is ready for anything.

DODDS: *I'm not a drinking man, but my nerves are in a terrible state ... terrible ...*

JOE has prepared the drink. He pushes it over as EGBERT observes:

EGBERT: *Nothing like a dash of the dog — and then if the whammies persist, a bit of the hair of the dog.*

The stranger does away with the drink without a blink and nods for an encore. EGBERT eyes him in appreciation.

EGBERT: *Not a drinking man, you say?*

DODDS: *Dodds is the name — Martin M. Dodds — and a man more beset by trouble you'll never see!*

He knocks off another Suisses, as he continues:

DODDS: *I'm manager of the Tel-Avis Productions, here on location — and our director shows up so jingled he sounds like all the reindeer in the world ... Have a drink.*

As the barman fixes them up, EGBERT speaks expansively.

EGBERT: *Motion pictures ... the galloping tintypes — the flicks — ah, now you are yodelling right up my canyon, Mr Dodds ... I directed Fatty Arbuckle, Buster Keaton, Flora Finch, and " Buying An Umbrella " in the old Sennett days ... you know ... John Bunny ... and at nights, I used to work as usher in the nickelodeon theatre on Alvarado Street . . . I guess that's why I just can't get the celluloid out of my blood.*

MR DODDS, now pretty well Suissesed, grasps at a straw.

DODDS : *Say . . . would you help us out?*

EGBERT : *Egbert Sousé, sir, was never one to turn a deaf ear to a cry of distress.*

DODDS : *Fine! Cooperation! That's what I like to hear from a man! Bartender — set 'em up again!*

EGBERT : *And that's what I like to hear from a man!*

As they beam appreciatively at each other.[15]

MYRTLE and OG approach the front of the Lompoc National Bank, where its sign is in evidence. Beneath is the added notation, *Hours 10-3.* OG is still impressed by EGBERT.

OG : *I didn't have any idea your father was quite like that!*

MYRTLE uneasily, yet defensively : *He's a little odd, all right, but he sort of grows on you . . .* Hastily she adds : *In a nice way, I mean.*

OG unexpectedly : *But I think he's nice already! Helpful and everything.*

MYRTLE relieved : *Yes, say what you will about Egbert Sousé, he's always ready to help! Well, here we are.*

They have come to the front of the bank. OG puts out his hand, which MYRTLE shakes.

OG : *Thanks for walking me down, Myrtle . . . See you tonight?*

MYRTLE : *If you want to.*

OG : *You know I do.*

MYRTLE giggles, frees her hand, and goes. OG looks after her, pleased.

As OG looks, his gaze fixes on something else off, and his eyes widen.

A fine car is driving down the street. EGBERT and MARTIN DODDS impressive in the back seat.

OG's smile deepens. It certainly looks as if he is going to have a swell father-in-law!

MAN'S VOICE : *Well, look at that!*

OG turns to a fellow CLERK, who is about to enter the front door. This local yokel is looking after the spectacle of the car going down the street bearing EGBERT. OG preens himself a little.

OG : *That is Mr Egbert Sousé.*

CLERK with a cackle : *I know — with an accent grave over the " e ".*

And cackling again he enters the bank. The laughter has disconcerted OG. He looks uncertainly in the direction EGBERT has gone, then puzzled, turns and goes into the bank.[16]

The Tel-Avis Motion Picture Company is on location. There are several trucks; sound trucks, lamp trucks, etc, and other essentials to the making of motion pictures. There is a bus, around which a dozen or more Western-garbed extras are standing. Sitting in lordly aloofness, on his chair, is the director, E. PISMO CLAM. He views all of these activities with the solemn expression only peculiar to a director who is boiled as an owl. At the moment someone is bringing him a cup of coffee.

The car arrives bearing EGBERT and DODDS. As they start to get out, the ASSISTANT DIRECTOR comes running up.

ASSISTANT DIRECTOR as he indicates off : *Still can't do a thing with him, Mr Dodds. He's tight as a snare drum.*

DODDS looks off with a fine production manager frown.

PISMO CLAM waves the coffee away with a regal gesture.

MR DODDS sniffs and indicates EGBERT.

DODDS : *We won't bother any more with him. Mr Sousé here, will take over the direction.*

ASSISTANT DIRECTOR : *Oh fine! Glad to meet you, Mr Sousé.*

EGBERT with befitting dignity : *You should be . . . Well, shall we proceed?*

DODDS admiringly, to the assistant : *You see? Right away he wants to get started. Let him have the script.*

EGBERT : *Oh, don't bother — don't bother.*

Both DODDS and the assistant are somewhat startled. But at this moment there is the sound of a car, off. The assistant indicates :

ASSISTANT DIRECTOR : *Here come Francois and Miss Plupp — our leads. I gave 'em a late call.*

EGBERT looking : *Hmm . . . I should say the later, the better.*

143

On the opposite side of the street a car has driven in with the leads — a very tall dark type and a small blonde ingenue. They both look like good players of road companies. As they get out of the car, EGBERT enters the scene.

EGBERT: *Good morning, thespians.*

They look at him a little surprised, but MR DODDS comes in immediately to make introductions.

DODDS: *Miss Plupp — Francois — this is Mr Sousé — our new director.*

EGBERT, looking from one to the other, naively inquires:

EGBERT lifting his hat to the ingenue: *This is Miss Plupp, I take it?* And to the man: *And you are Francois? Did you have a good sleep last night?*[17]

FRANCOIS dramatically: *Comme ci, comme ca. I was up most of the night studying. I slept with the script under my pillow the way we used to do in the old stock days. I don't know whether this part is suited to my personality or not.*

EGBERT: *Don't give it a thought. I've changed the whole script. We're using one that I've had in moth balls for years — always carry it with me in case of emergency. You'll love it. Instead of being an English drawing room drayma, I've made it a circus picture.*

CLAM reacts to this.

Back to FRANCOIS and EGBERT.

FRANCOIS: *One, two or three rings?*

EGBERT, thinking he is facetious, puts him in his place.

EGBERT: *One ring and a side show.*

DODDS, still in a friendly haze, is enchanted with EGBERT. He turns to the SCRIPT GIRL and says quickly:

DODDS: *Don't just sit there — take down everything he says!*

As she starts to obey . . .

Back to EGBERT and FRANCOIS.

EGBERT: *You play a young college boy. It's Saturday afternoon — You make touchdown after touchdown.*

EGBERT continuing: *You kick goals . . . you make passes (but not at the heroine) . . . you make the longest run with the ball ever made . . . and it's in the rain.*[18]

EGBERT, in illustrating to the actors what they're supposed to do, accidentally sits on the SCRIPT GIRL's lap.

144

CLAM is beginning to burn.

EGBERT gets up and says to the SCRIPT GIRL :[19]

EGBERT : *I beg your pardon . . . It's in the rain . . . you play with rubber boots on . . . never been done before in pictures . . . original . . . we can get some great gags . . . fish coming out of the boots, or maybe boots coming out of fish. The circus comes to town. It's raining felines and canines. It gets on fire or is struck by lightning or something. Naturally, they can't give a show. Maybe the wind blows the tent over. You, Miss Plupp, play the bearded lady with the circus.*

MISS PLUPP looking at him, askance : *I play who?*

EGBERT : *Wait a minute. Hold your thought. He sees you in the fifty dollar seats. He immediately falls in love with you. He can't take his eyes off you.*

MISS PLUPP : *How can he play base . . .?*

EGBERT : *Foot.*

MISS PLUPP : *. . . football, and watch me in the grandstand?*

EGBERT : *It's part of the plot. Then here comes the twist. The opposite team wins by a country mile on account of him not keeping his mind on the race . . . or . . . game. The coach knocks Francois insensible with a goal post? You run down and soothe his aching head. It's a case of love at first sight.*

CLAM is now holding his head.

We go back to EGBERT and the actors.

MISS PLUPP : *He falls in love with me and I got whiskers on?*

EGBERT : *He has astigmatism. We insert a short scene showing him groping around in an oculist's office, kicking over chairs and things . . .barking his shins . . . stepping in the spittoon and everything. Another thing, you're so far away he can't see the whiskers. Anyway, it is only a short beard . . . a Van Dyke . . . you know what a Van Dyke is?*

MISS PLUPP indignantly : *I certainly do!*

EGBERT : *Fine. And now he is just half dazed . . . he can't see anything. He only remembers you as he saw you in the grandstand. " Will you marry me if I heal up?" he says. You say, " Yeah ". You go off to the local barber shop, get shaved and play the rest of the picture with an absolutely clean face — lipstick, eyebrows, rouge and pedicure.*[20]

Meanwhile, MRS BRUNCH, AGATHA and ELSIE MAE push

through the crowd to see what's going on. They all see EGBERT at once. ELSIE MAE lets out a yelp.

MRS BRUNCH: *It's him!*

AGATHA: *Well, for the . . .!*

The ASSISTANT DIRECTOR looks at them with a scowl.

ASSISTANT DIRECTOR: *Quiet, please!*

As the two stare pop-eyed, obeying.[21]

We return to EGBERT and MISS PLUPP.

MISS PLUPP: *Say . . . don't I have a child to cry over or something?*

EGBERT: *Sure, sure . . . a little girl about twelve.*

MISS PLUPP: *For gosh sakes . . . how old am I supposed to be?*

EGBERT: *Don't let it worry you . . . we'll fix it with make-up.*

EGBERT turns round and surveys the crowd. Then he sees his family.[22]

EGBERT: *Ah, the very little girl. Come here, my puppet.*

We see MRS BRUNCH, AGATHA and ELSIE MAE.

ELSIE MAE: *He didn't know me!*

MRS BRUNCH: *Drinking again!*

EGBERT enters to them, takes ELSIE MAE's hand.

EGBERT: *You'd like to act in the movies, wouldn't you?*

ELSIE MAE starts to pull away, but he holds her tight and whispers fiercely:

EGBERT: *Didn't you ever hear of Shirley Durbin?*

He walks her toward the actors.

PISMO CLAM is now no longer able to contain himself.

PISMO CLAM: *A moppet!*

With an anguished cry he leaps to his feet and he goes over to the group, crying:

PISMO CLAM: *Not in my picture — never!*[23]

CLAM hands EGBERT a cigar.

CLAM: *I will carry on now. Goodbye, and thank you for your trouble.*

EGBERT: *Oh, nothing at all — nothing at all. Always glad to be of any slight assistance.*

DODDS is standing with the SCRIPT GIRL.

DODDS drily: *I guess our genius is okay again.*

GIRL: *What'll I do with these notes I took when Mr Sousé was directing.*

146

DODDS : *Send 'em in with the day's report. Shows somebody was working around here!*[24]

As CLAM turns to talk to the actors, ELSIE MAE indicates that she has been bitten by ambition. She hauls off and kicks CLAM on the shins.

ELSIE MAE : *I wanna be in the pitcher!*

CLAM's reaction is quick and definite. He punches ELSIE MAE on the nose. The kid backs away in surprise. EGBERT takes CLAM's hand.

EGBERT : *Sir, you are a man after my own heart!*

Then raising his hat, he walks away.

CLAM looks after him, a little surprised. Then into the shot sails a rock and bangs his head. As stunned, he looks off. ELSIE MAE is running down the street, her score evened.[25]

Walking along, EGBERT comes to the car with the now enraged CHAUFFEUR working on it. The little old LADY is sitting quietly in the back seat, as before. EGBERT lifts his hat politely to her, and nods graciously. As he goes past the CHAUFFEUR, EGBERT says :

EGBERT : *Haven't you fixed that yet?*

As the CHAUFFEUR straightens up, a wrench in his hand and murder in his heart, EGBERT scuttles quickly on.[26]

EGBERT comes happily to the door of the Black Pussy Cat, starts to push it open. It is locked. He looks at it, annoyed.

INSERT :

> *Out to Lunch*
> *Joe*

EGBERT makes a frustrated gesture. He turns around and looks off.

A pretty GIRL sitting on a bus bench, revealing a charming expanse of hosiery. She is reading a book.

EGBERT's face brightens and he goes over to the bench. He is humming gaily.

As EGBERT comes to the GIRL he lifts his hat.

EGBERT : *May I share this bench with you?*

GIRL : *It's bus property.*

147

He sits down.

EGBERT : *Lovely weather we're having.*

GIRL coldly : *It was.*

EGBERT gives a take at the way history is repeating itself. A car bearing a young man comes by and stops. The GIRL smiles at him.

YOUNG MAN : *Going my way?*

The GIRL puts down the book and gets up, enters the car. He drives away as EGBERT watches in fascination. He picks up the book.

INSERT :

HOW TO WIN FRIENDS AND INFLUENCE PEOPLE

EGBERT : *There must be something in this, after all!*

EGBERT very carefully takes out his handkerchief and dusts off the bench. He then spreads the handkerchief and sits down to read. Just as he does so the wheel of a passing car hits a puddle and splashes all over him. As he looks angrily after the car . . .

One of the CROOKS is driving.

FIRST CROOK : *What's in this here bank besides old street car transfers?*

SECOND CROOK : *There's a movie company in town, and you know what their payrolls are.*

FIRST CROOK : *No, but I'm willing to find out.*

SECOND CROOK : *Okay then, pull up here, and leave the motor running.*[27]

The car pulls up outside the bank. The men get out, glance around furtively, and walk swiftly into the bank.

Inside the bank : at the right hand side are two cashiers' windows : receiving teller and paying teller. The bank is small. Two doors from rear are offices, and a desk in recess near the entrance. There are several people in the bank. One receiving tellers' window is handled by a man who wears a straw hat with no crown. The paying teller is OG. One of the crooks goes to OG's window and stands behind a patron, as though waiting his turn. The other loiters by, watching.

Outside the bank: a pair of annoyed POLICEMEN are examining the CROOKS' car, which is parked along the curb on which is printed: *No Parking.*

FIRST COP: *Parked in a loading zone with his engine running, eh?*

SECOND COP: *Guess we better just take it over to headquarters.*

They start to get into the car.

At the teller's window: the gunmen now points a revolver at OG.

FIRST CROOK: *Reach!*

The other, also brandishing a revolver, covers the small group in the bank.

SECOND CROOK: *All right, everybody — it's a stick-up!*

As he says this, a woman screams, faints, falls against a lady with a fat boy. She in turn falls against the boy and the whole group falls on the floor.

The crook reaches through the window and grabs several meticulously arranged and counted bundles of bills, securely held together with rubber bands.

CROOK tucking bills into his coat pocket: *Now keep your foot off that alarm!*

He turns and starts out.

The robbers run from the bank. OG, reminded of the alarm, now jams his foot down on it. The bell sounds.

The CROOKS emerge from the bank. They look up and down the street. To their bewilderment, they find their car is not in front of the bank where they left it. They start hurriedly up the street. The bell sounds behind them.

The CROOKS go up street and disappear into an alley, starting to run as they do so.

As OG and several men run out of the bank, the bell clamoring wildly.

OG: *Police! Police! A hold-up!*

The COPS are driving along in the CROOKS' car. Now they hear the sound of the cries and the bell behind them.

COP: *Sounds like trouble at the bank!*

He starts to turn the car back.

The CROOKS are in alley. The two are excited and alarmed.

FIRST CROOK: *Let's cut this money up right now.*

SECOND CROOK: *Keep going!*

First Crook : *Suppose we get split up?*

Second Crook : *What's the matter . . . don't you trust me?*

First Crook : *I don't trust nobody!*

He grabs the other by the lapel of his coat.

First Crook : *Then give me half of that dough!*

The other refuses to give up the money. They are still fighting as they hasten out of sight.

Egbert is rattling the door of the Black Pussy Cat café in vain.

The Cops draw up to curb outside the bank. Og leaps to the side of the car and hangs on.

Teller pointing towards alley : *Bank robbers . . . two of them . . . they ran into the alley!*

As the car starts off, with the Cops sounding the horn full blast.[28]

Outside the Black Pussy Cat, centering on alley behind bench, taking in Egbert returning to the bench.[29] He is looking back at the door of the saloon muttering in annoyance. Just then the two Crooks race out of the alley, the one with the money in the lead. The other belts him with a pistol butt and he folds behind the bench just as Egbert, his back still turned, sits down on it again and picks up his book. Before the Second Crook has had time to take the money from his partner, the sound of the horn blast of the car carrying the Cops and Og approaches. Panicky, the Crook starts to run. He runs out towards street in front of Egbert. As he passes him, he tosses his gun away. Egbert hears horn, mutters " Quiet, please," and goes on reading.

The gun hits Egbert's book, knocks it into his chest. Egbert goes over backward, carrying the bench with him.

Egbert, Crook and the bench are enmeshed on sidewalk. The car with the Cops and Og speeds up. Egbert pulls himself out of the entanglement. Still dazed, he is sitting on the fallen Crook's back. He unconsciously clings to revolver. The two Cops get out of the car, grab Egbert but Og recognizes him.[30]

150

OG : *He isn't one of them — he's Mr Souse.*

EGBERT : *Sousé — accent grave over the " e ".*

The COP sees the money on the fallen CROOK.

FIRST COP : *Got him — money and all!*

SECOND COP : *Good work, Mr Sousé.*

EGBERT is most bewildered.

EGBERT : *Yeah — yeah.*

OG : *The other fellow got away on you, eh, Mr Sousé?*

EGBERT : *Yes he did, after pulling a knife on me that long . . . an assagai.*

TELLER : *Lucky you had your gun on you. Always carry one?*

EGBERT noticing revolver in his hand for first time, sheepishly : *Yeh — my trusty pistol never leaves my side. Even pick my teeth with it.*

OG : *Just wait till the people at the bank hear about this!*

The COPS put the bracelets on the dazed CROOK and put him in the car. One of them says to OG :

COP : *You better come along to headquarters with us.*

As OG starts to get into the car, he turns to EGBERT.

OG : *Myrtle should be awfully proud to have a father like you, Mr Sousé.*

EGBERT graciously : *Always glad to be of any slight assistance.*

Quite a crowd has gathered to watch as the police car drives off.

EGBERT is now the center of an admiring group, among whom are several kids. JOE, the belated bartender, comes into scene and asks a KID :

JOE : *What's the matter?*[31]

KID : *Elsie Mae Adele Brunch Sousé's father just caught a burglar who tried to cut his throat with a knife that big — and he shot him, or something. You oughta see the pistol he carries!*

JOE impressed : *You don't say?*

KID : *Did you get him with one bullet, Mr Souse?*

EGBERT : *Sousé, boys . . . accent grave over the " e " . . . No bullets, son — just my bare hands.*[32]

ANOTHER KID : *Will you sign my autograph book?*

EGBERT : *Gladly, my little ragamuffin!* He signs.

JOE pushes his way into the shot.

JOE : *Pulled a knife on you, eh?*

EGBERT: *Joseph, the sword that Lee surrendered to Grant was a potato peeler by comparison.*

JOE: *Say, you better come in and have a little poultice on the house.*[33]

EGBERT with dignity: *Thanks, my belated friend. But I must repair to the bosom of my family. Worried about me, they doubtless are, after this fracas.*

> EGBERT is about to leave the group — with JOE open-mouthed at his refusal of a drink — when a REPORTER enters briskly.

REPORTER: *Mr Sousé, I'm Dolan of the Lompoc Beagle. I'd like . . .*

EGBERT: *Very well, son — phone your editor to tear out the whole front page! I'll give you a story that'll rip this town wide open!*

> As they start off, the REPORTER says aggrievedly:

REPORTER: *You been going to the movies too, Mr Sousé?*

> The REPORTER and EGBERT walk away down the street.

EGBERT: *Exclusive to the Lompoc Beagle: In a sensational display of courage, Egbert Sousé, prominent citizen and father of Myrtle Sousé of this city, today routed a pair of ferocious criminals with larcenous intentions toward the lettuce of the National Bank . . .*

> They pass the car with the little old LADY. Now *she* is out working on the engine. The CHAUFFEUR sits exhaustedly in the rear seat. EGBERT tips his hat to *him* and walks on, still full of himself. The REPORTER is hastily taking notes.[34]

EGBERT: *Drawing his own revolver, which he carries for such emergencies, he struck the felon — said to be the notorious Repulsive Rogan — over the head with the butt of his trusty weapon, felling him to the earth.*

> A MAN passes and interrupts the flight of his fancy.

MAN: *When you going to pay me that dollar, Egbert?*

EGBERT: *Hello, George.* He continues his interview. *The other ruffian, alleged to be Filthy McNasty — known as The Wild Cat, and wanted in every state in and out of the Union — swung an assagai of razor-edge sharpness at Mr Sousé's neck.*

> A kid rushes up with an autograph book.

BOY: *Sign my book, Mr Sousé?*

EGBERT as he does so: *Certainly, son — no trouble at all.*

> EGBERT goes on to the REPORTER.

EGBERT: *Mr Sousé, who claims the distinction of fighting a draw* with John L. Sullivan in a back bar room in 1896, dodged the blow and kicked Filthy McNasty in the kidneys. McNasty ran down Lompoc Boulevard screaming with pain. He is still at large — minus a kidney.

EGBERT tips his hat to the REPORTER.

EGBERT continuing : *Good day, Mr Dolan.*

REPORTER stunned : *Good day.*

EGBERT goes on hippily, by himself. He shadow boxes and just misses an old lady's jaw, as she turns the corner.

She screams; he bows.

EGBERT : *I too am startled, milady. For the first time a newspaper is going to get a story right!*

He continues down the street.

EGBERT is signing autographs with a flourish. The last of the kids thanks EGBERT — the hero — and runs off to join his companions. EGBERT approaches the gate to his house.

As he reaches the gate, two men with books and holding pencils approach him. EGBERT obligingly signs, tips his hat and walks up path.

They are stunned.

FIRST MAN : *My gosh, that fellow makes quick decisions! I sold him a set of encyclopedias, just like that!*

SECOND MAN : *That's nothing. I sold him a grand piano!*

As they look respectfully toward the house.[35]

MRS SOUSÉ and MRS BRUNCH are seated at the table playing Chinese checkers. A plate of nuts is at their elbows and they are munching toast and drinking tea. Toast is dry. EGBERT enters, anxious to tell of his exploit.[36]

EGBERT : *A good, good afternoon to you ladies . . .*

MRS SOUSE : *For heaven's sake, Egbert — can't you see we're busy?*

EGBERT : *But I wanted to tell you . . .*

MRS BRUNCH sarcastically : *We know all about how you directed the picture.*

EGBERT airily : *Oh, that's water over the mill race . . . Since then I've been busy catching a thief who stole two million dollars from the Lompoc National Bank.*

MRS BRUNCH sniffs, but doesn't look up from her game.

MRS BRUNCH : *You would! — The Lompoc National!* He speaks

153

to Agatha. *Those are the shylocks that hold the mortgage on this house, ain't they? I'm sorry they didn't get away with the whole crooked bank. Leave it to Egbert — he would do a thing like that!*[37]

MRS SOUSE: *For goodness sake, Egbert, if you're going to help out a bank, why not pick a nice one?*

EGBERT naively: *Well, er — it seemed like a good idea at the time.*

MRS BRUNCH: *All your ideas seem good at the time — but they ain't.*

Although he might have expected it, EGBERT is disgruntled by the reception his news begot.

EGBERT: *But everybody was talking about it — why, even Joe wanted to give me a drink.*

MRS BRUNCH sarcastically: *And I suppose you turned him down.*

EGBERT as though surprised at himself: *Why, yes, I did.*

MRS BRUNCH: *I bet! It's your move, Agatha.*

EGBERT: *I signed autograph books and everything.*

MRS SOUSE: *Egbert, will you please be quiet. Don't you see we're concentrating.*

The two women are leaning over the game, as before. As EGBERT starts out, MRS BRUNCH is saying:

MRS BRUNCH: *No consideration — absolutely none at all!*

As EGBERT comes out the door he tries to get back into his former mood.

EGBERT: *Just wait till they see those newspapers — "Prominent Citizen Routs Raspacallians Single-handed. Egbert Sousé, sportsman, bon-vivant and father of Myrtle Sousé."*

MYRTLE'S VOICE: *Dad — oh, Dad!*

EGBERT starts, called out of his pleasant absorption.

MYRTLE comes running up on the porch. She is excited and delighted.

MYRTLE: *I'm so excited — I think it's simply wonderful. Imagine — a hero right in our own family!*

EGBERT pleased, but modest: *So word of that little fracas is being bruted about, is it?*

MYRTLE: *I stopped in the bank to say hello to Og — and he says Mr Skinner, the president, wants you to drop in for a reward!*

EGBERT: *A reward, eh? Fancy that. Goes to show you that righteous living pays. Yes, indeed. And just when shall I do this afore-*

mentioned dropping?

MYRTLE : *He said whenever it's convenient for you.*

EGBERT : *Well, it so happens I'm not doing anything just at the moment . . . I might as well look in on Mr Skinner.*

MYRTLE : *Oh, I'm so thrilled! Have you told mother?*

EGBERT frowning : *Yes, but perhaps I understated things a bit. If you care to, you might tell her — and your grandmother — what they are saying about me in the byways and highways of the town — over smart luncheon tables and in luxurious clubs.*

He raises his hat and starts off.

MYRTLE : *Let me know what happens.*

EGBERT : *You may depend upon it, my pet.*

As he goes blithely down the walk.

The car at the sidewalk : the old LADY is now as greasy as the CHAUFFEUR. As EGBERT comes along, full of himself and speculations upon the coming reward, she looks up grimly. EGBERT passes by. The old LADY raises a wrench, lets it fly. EGBERT gets the wrench on the back of the head. He groans and looks around.

He sees the little old LADY, angry as a wet hen, as she shakes her fist at him. EGBERT nods and raises his hat.

EGBERT : *I get your point.*

He then turns and continues his progress.[38]

Shooting towards the entrance of the bank : EGBERT is entering. He removes his hat, holds it in his hand. He goes to receiving TELLER's window.

EGBERT to TELLER : *I have an appointment with Mr Skinner.*

As he says this, a customer pushes his way in between him and the TELLER. Customer finishes his business quickly. EGBERT tries again. Another customer gets to window.

TELLER to EGBERT : *Step aside, please . . .*

Customer finishes his business; EGBERT steps in again. A little old lady comes to window.

TELLER in more commanding tone, to EGBERT : *Step aside, please — just a moment.*

EGBERT waits. Customer finishes business. TELLER takes his name plate from window, replaces it with a sign reading :

Next Window Please.

We move to the SECOND TELLER's window. He is the one wearing a straw hat without a crown. EGBERT enters scene. He goes to window.

EGBERT: *Good morning.*

EGBERT and the TELLER face each other.

TELLER: *How are you, sir?*

EGBERT feeling better at having gained attention: *Oh — as well as can be expected after the tussle I had with those bandits. I just came from the doctor and he told me I would probably have to have my gall bladder and tonsils removed because of the fight and saving the bank all that dough — and also a slight appendectomy.*

A coloured man, MOSES, enters the scene.

TELLER: *Just a minute, please.*

EGBERT steps back.[39]

MOSES: *Mawnin', sah. Ah'd like to draw mah money out of the bank.*

TELLER: *Why? Are you going to make some sort of an investment?*

EGBERT pushing himself in: *When I saw my doctor and endrocologist they said I had a slipped sacroiliac, Vincent's disease and a stubborn case of dipsomania due to this encounter.*[40]

MOSES also talking to TELLER: *Ah ain't gonna make no investment.*

TELLER waving EGBERT aside, to MOSES: *You're not going to close your account with us, are you?*

MOSES: *Yes, Ah am.*

EGBERT: *Moestine, Gilhooley & Muffington want to take my case on a 75-25 per cent contingency basis . . . winner take all.*

TELLER to MOSES: *Is there any particular reason?*

MOSES: *Ah'm kinda skeered.*

TELLER: *What are you afraid of, Moses?*

MOSES: *Well, everytime Ah come in here, you got that hat on and you look as though you're ready to leave any minute. It makes me nervous.*

TELLER: *Oh. I just wear this hat on account of a little hayfever.*

OG enters to the baffled EGBERT.[41]

EGBERT and OG together.

OG: *Good morning, Mr Sousé — I've been looking for you.*

EGBERT: *That is where you and this zombie . . .* He indicates the

156

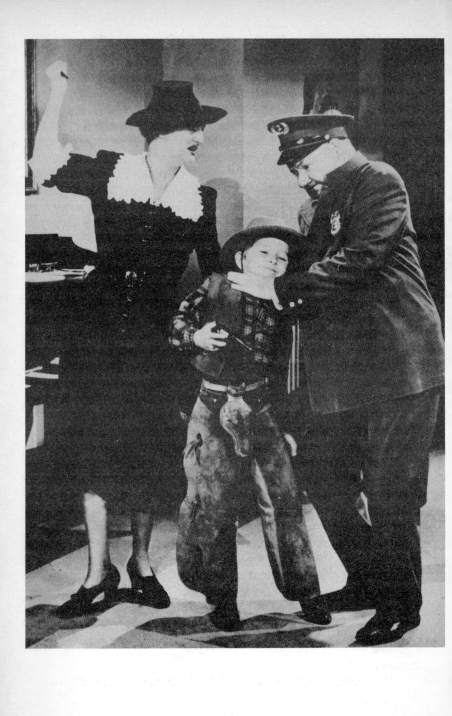

TELLER ... *differ sharply!*

OG: *Mr Skinner is expecting you — his office is right over there.*

EGBERT: *Thank you, Og. I think I can manage to totter that far.*

He gives the TELLER a final glare.

EGBERT: *Hayfever — I'm not surprised!*

He exits.

EGBERT enters SKINNER'S office, places his hat on the rack, walks towards the desk at which SKINNER is seated, dictating to a very pretty STENOGRAPHER. (She is the girl of the bus bench.)

EGBERT walks towards desk, getting over the fact he is looking at girl's legs, which are crossed and showing plenty of exposure. As she sees EGBERT staring at them she jumps up, places her notebook on the desk. Her pencil falls on floor.

STENOGRAPHER to SKINNER: *Will that be all?*

SKINNER: *Just a moment, please.*

Girl stoops over to retrieve pencil. It has rolled under a chair, and she turns her back towards EGBERT as she bends over. EGBERT is giving her a good double " o ".

SKINNER: *Young Oggilby has told me of your heroism, Mr Sousé.*

EGBERT still intent on girl: *Oh, nothing at all — nothing at all.*

SKINNER: *To the contrary, I should say! You showed exceptional bravery.*

EGBERT'S eyes are still on the girl, who is now trying to reach under heavy chair for pencil.

EGBERT: *Yes, I did . . . yes . . . yes . . . that's right. As a matter of fact, it is quite exceptional — quite . . .*

Still eyeing the girl. She finds pencil, stands up.

EGBERT continuing: *. . . it required cool nerves and grit . . . and if I have anything, I have grit.* He is actually talking to the girl. *In my school days, my chums used to call me " Gritty " — " Gritty Sousé ". Catching those crooks was due to my athletic training in my not-so-long-ago younger days.*

Girl flops down into chair, crosses her legs, thinks better of it, tries to pull down her skirts.

EGBERT: *I used to have the figure of Apollo Belvedere . . . golden hair that hung to my knees. I was known as Young Curlilocks, or Killer Claude.*

Girl twists her chair so as not to be directly facing EGBERT.

161

EGBERT : *It wouldn't take me two days to get right back in that same condition again, if I took a little exercise and laid off sen-sen.*

Girl has now turned her chair until she is facing sideways. EGBERT walks around it to hold his view.

EGBERT : *Fought Sullivan 108 rounds to a draw in Oswego, New York, on the 4th of July. Everyone said I was robbed of the decision.*

STENOGRAPHER is trying to turn back again.

SKINNER writing, uninterested : *Remarkable . . . remarkable.*

EGBERT following girl's legs around, addresses her : *Haven't I met you somewhere before?*

STENOGRAPHER curtly : *No.*

EGBERT : *Did anyone ever tell you, you were a ringer for the girl that was chosen as Miss Punksatawnee last year in Atlantic City?*

STENOGRAPHER getting up, interrupting him : *Yes!*

She starts out of scene, as SKINNER gets up and comes out from behind desk.

The girl walks to the door, SKINNER on one side, bows and clicks his heels. EGBERT, seeing this, does likewise, removes his hat from the rack and tips it deferentially, replaces it on the rack. The girl goes out, slamming the door.⁴²

SKINNER and EGBERT are left together.

SKINNER : *Now, Mr Sousé, we want to show our appreciation of your gallantry and daring.*

EGBERT : *Oh, thank you . . . thank you . . .*

SKINNER : *I wish to personally give you a hearty handclasp.*

EGBERT less gratefully : *Well, thank you, thank you . . .*

SKINNER : *And present you, with the company's compliments, one of our 1940 calendars.*

SKINNER reaches up and takes calendar from the wall and hands it to EGBERT.⁴³

EGBERT taking it, looks at it. It is possibly a nude figure of a girl standing near a lake, her back turned : *Thank you, thank you, thank you . . . doesn't look unlike the Mona Lisa . . .*

SKINNER affectionately taking him by the arm : *Will you have a seat?*

He leads EGBERT toward desk.

EGBERT takes a seat and SKINNER moves around desk to his chair, talking as he moves.⁴⁴

SKINNER: *Mr Sousé, our board of directors have decided to offer you a position.*

EGBERT: *Hear, hear!*

SKINNER: *The remuneration at first will be small but there are many chances for advancement. Who knows but within a short period of time you may be vice-president — my first and only vice.*

He gives a corny, hail-fellow laugh. EGBERT laughs with him. Then his face straightens abruptly and he asks:

EGBERT: *What's the job?*

SKINNER: *One for which, in view of your record today, we feel you are singularly fitted. We want you for our special officer.*

EGBERT: *Oh, a bank dick.*

SKINNER coldly: *I believe the underworld refers to the post as that.*

EGBERT hastily: *I don't know where I could have picked up the phrase — in passing a poolroom, perhaps . . . Special officer — ah yes, that will be indeed an interesting experience.*

SKINNER: *Then we'll consider it settled . . . Oh yes, naturally we will deduct a certain amount from your salary each week which will pay off the interest of the mortgage on your home.*

EGBERT a little uneasily: *Oh, naturally — naturally. Mortgage — interest — high finance — fine. Feel like a vice-president already —*

SKINNER crosses to open a closet to take out a uniform. As camera pans with him, he says:

SKINNER: *Fortunately our former officer, Mr Thomas, was almost your size. This uniform should be a perfect fit on you.*

EGBERT startled: *Thomas? Wasn't he the fellow who was . . .?*

He makes a shooting motion with his finger. SKINNER holds up the uniform and nods.

SKINNER: *Yes, but look — the bullet holes have been mended so well they are invisible.*

EGBERT looking at it: *And so is Thomas!*

SKINNER shakes out the uniform, saying enthusiastically:

SKINNER: *I can see you in that uniform, bright and early tomorrow morning, attending to your duties — a man of conscientious morals and unquestioned courage — a credit to the community!*

As he drops the uniform on EGBERT, who looks somewhat baffled by the spot he has got himself on.[45]

EGBERT is wearing the uniform, and quite proudly.[46]

We now see that EGBERT is at the bar of the Black Pussy Cat having a poultice and talking to JOE.

EGBERT : ... *a credit to the community, Mr. Skinner said I was — a man of conscientious morals and unquestioned courage.*

JOE, polishing a glass, emits a snort.

EGBERT : *Why the rude remark! You've never heard my courage questioned, have you?*

JOE : *Questioned? I've never heard it mentioned!*

EGBERT grumbling : *Joe, I fear that the sour wine of cynicism runs in your veins ... Called me in, Skinner did, and said, " Write your own ticket ". You learn the business right ... Special officer, that's me. Bank dick in underworld parlance. But after all I haven't even ...* He glances at his watch ... *started to work yet.*

WATERBURY sidles closer to EGBERT, offers his card, and begins passionately to spout :

WATERBURY : *Pardon me, but I couldn't help overhearing your conversation. My name is Waterbury and I'm in the Bond and Stock Business. I'm up here for my health. I like the little town and I'd like to make some contacts. I think you are the very man. I have five thousand shares in the Beefsteak Mines in Leapfrog, Nevada, that I would like to turn over to your bank. The shares are now selling for ten cents a share. Telephone sold for five cents a share. These are twice as expensive, consequently, they will become twice as valuable — naturally — you are not a dunce. Telephone is now listed at one hundred and seventy-three dollars and you can't buy it. Three thousand, four hundred and sixty dollars for every nickel they put in it ... The point I am trying to make is this — These shares are selling for ten cents. It's simple arithmetic — if five gets you ten, ten will get you twenty. Sixteen cylinder cars — large home in the city — balconies upstairs and down — home in the country — big trees, private golf course — streams flow through the rear of the estate — warm summer afternoon fishing under the cool trees drinking ice-cold beer, and eating ham and cheese on rye —*[47]

EGBERT interestedly : *With mustard?*

WATERBURY : *Yeh — the man pulls in through the shaded drive in an armoured car from the bank — dumps a basket of coupons worth hundred of thousands of dollars — says, " Sign here, please, on the dotted line," and is off (to the soft chirping of our little*

164

feathered friends through the arboreal dell). That's what these bonds mean! I'd rather part with my beloved grandmother's paisley shawl or her wedding ring than part with these bonds. He heatedly removes a handkerchief from his pocket, wipes his eyes, stomps his foot on floor. *Gosh! Pardon my language . . . I feel like a dog. It's got to be done . . . now or never. Take it or leave it.*[48]

EGBERT convinced at last : *Well — drop in and see me at the Lompoc National in about an hour.*

WATERBURY : *Fine — fine, I'll be there.*

He shakes hands with EGBERT, a firm clasp which almost breaks EGBERT's hand.

EGBERT : *A hearty handclasp to bind the bargain.*

He starts to go, feeling his fingers and mutters :

EGBERT continuing : *Too hearty.*

WATERBURY : *You think you can raise the money all right?*

EGBERT loftily : *I work in a bank, don't I?*

As he sweeps out.

Shooting towards street on EGBERT as he enters the bank, filled with importance, proud of uniform. He salutes right and left to various people coming in and out.

We follow EGBERT as he makes his salutes.

EGBERT : *Good morning . . . good morning . . .*

No one pays any attention to him. EGBERT moves on towards OG's cage.

EGBERT comes to OG.

EGBERT : *Greetings, my lad.*

OG : *Good morning, Mr Sousé. Ready to go, eh?*

EGBERT : *Ready? Say, I'm gone! Og, my boy, I've got you set for life! I don't hang around these bars for nothing. I just met a poor fellow who is in trouble. There's something the matter with his grandmother's paisley shawl. He has five thousand shares of stock in the Beefsteak Mines and you can buy them for a handful of hay.*

OG : *Hay?*

EGBERT : *Ten cents a share. You've heard of the telephone company, light — gas — they sold for five cents a share. How would you like something better for ten cents a share? Beautiful home in the city. Upstairs and down. Beer flowing through the estate.*[49]

OG : *Beer?*

EGBERT : *Fishing — trees — a man comes up from the bar and dumps three thousand, four hundred and sixty dollars in your lap for every nickel invested, says, "Sign Here," and disappears through the waving fields of alfalfa.*

OG : *Do you feel all right, Mr Sousé?*

EGBERT : *Sure, I feel all right.*

OG a bit uncertainly : *Don't you think maybe you'd better keep out of that Black Pussy Cat place?*

EGBERT : *Listen, Og, I'm all excited. This fellow wants to settle down here. He's got to get rid of these shares. He sobbed like a child at the thought of disposing of them. How does this bank make it's money? By investing. Telephone sold for five cents a share and now you can't buy it for three thousand, five hundred dollars a share. You don't want to work in this bank all your life. You've got to take a chance. Take it while you're young. My uncle who was a Balloon Ascensionist jumped out of the basket of a balloon one day three and one-half miles in the air. He took a chance on landing on a load of hay.*[50]

OG : *Gosh! . . . Did he make it?*

EGBERT : *No. And that's the point. He waited too late in life. Had he been a younger man, he would have probably made it. So don't wait too long to take your chance in life. Don't make Myrtle a young man's slave. You want her to be happy, don't you.*[51]

OG : *Yes, but the fact is — I haven't the money. Of course, my bonus comes due in four days — seven hundred dollars.*[52]

EGBERT : *It's fate — that's what! You aren't one to die and leave your wife and children paupers! Borrow the seven hundred dollars from the bank. You can pay it back to the bank when your bonus comes up. You're not a jobber-nowl, Oggie! You're not a mooncalf! You're not a luddy duddy.*

OG wavering : *Well, I've never done anything like that before . . .*

EGBERT : *Tell me, my hesitant friend — how does the bank make its money? By taking the customer's money and lending it out. That's what you're doing, and instead of paying it back in thirty or sixty days, you're paying it back in five days.*

OG hesitates, then gives in, pounds on the desk : *Well, if you're sure — all right! Send him in.*

EGBERT: *Fine! My boy, I already feel that we own this paltry bank!*

> A dignified LADY with a young BOY enters the bank. The BOY is dressed in cowboy suit, carrying a toy revolver in a holster. EGBERT comes toward them. As he turns and eyes it like stout CORTEZ looking upon the Pacific . . .[53]
>
> Close shot of EGBERT, LADY and BOY.

EGBERT in commanding voice: *Madam, is that gun loaded?*

> The LADY draws herself up stiffly,[54] looks him over with cold disdain, and in a very dignified, cultured voice says:

LADY: *Scram!*

> EGBERT reacts to this, but holds his ground.

EGBERT pointing to child's gun: *Pardon me . . . is that revolver loaded?*

LADY with a sniff: *No, but I think you are!*

> She takes the child away.[55]
>
> A series of quick cuts follows to designate a busy banking day:

> PAPER MONEY IS BEING COUNTED.
> PASSBOOK ENTRIES BEING MADE.
> A BRINK'S TRUCK BEING LOADED.
> VAULT LOCK BEING GUIDED.
> COINS BEING ROLLED IN PAPER.
> MAN WRITING CHECK.

> EGBERT is watching, to his discomfiture.
>
> We see OG handing WATERBURY, the blue-sky-man, a handful of money and receiving stock certificates. EGBERT standing by, beams approvingly.
>
> The last of these short shots is of a shade being pulled behind the glass door. The shade is lettered " Bank Closed ".
>
> We find that it is EGBERT who is drawing the shade. Just as he does so, the door is pushed open to reveal a very dignified gentleman wearing a pince nez with black ribbon, conservative haberdashery, and carrying a briefcase. It is impossible, of course, to tell immediately who he is, but he has trouble written all over him.
>
> EGBERT is speaking to the newcomer with a befitting dignity.

EGBERT: *Sorry, friend, you didn't make it.*

NEWCOMER : *Just a minute, please.*

As EGBERT tries to close the door, newcomer takes card from his pocket, hands it to EGBERT. EGBERT takes the card, looks at it.

INSERT :

J. GEORGE JOHNSON
BANK EXAMINER[56]

EGBERT is electrified.

JOHNSON : *I would like to see Mr Skinner, please.*

EGBERT nervously : *Yes, yes — Mr Skinner. I'm awfully sorry, but he went out to the golf course on business and he won't be back until midnight. If he does happen in earlier, I'll give you a buzz. Where are you stopping?*

JOHNSON : *I'm stopping at the New Old Lompoc House.*

EGBERT : *Lovely weather we're having, nevertheless.*

JOHNSON turning away : *I'll be in for a check-up in the morning.*

EGBERT : *Good idea. Have one twice a year myself, regular as the swallows. Thought I might have a little bit of liver trouble — but they can't find it at all!*[57]

Despite his friendliness, the examiner merely nods and leaves. EGBERT looks worried. He looks at the card again. Then he goes quickly over to OG's cage.

EGBERT clearing his throat : *I have some bad news for you, my boy. Can you take it now, or would you like me to prepare you with an aspirin?*

OG alarmed : *What is it? What's happened?*

EGBERT hands him the card. OG reads it and moans.

OG : *The bank examiner!*

OG is agitated. He throws down a bundle of currency, which hits a feathered quill balanced on an inkwell. Quill soars into air, describes an arc, comes down point first on EGBERT's head, making him look like an Indian Chief.[58]

OG : *I might have known that would happen!*

EGBERT wrestling with quill in his hair : *Don't get excited — keep cool!*

OG : *Cool! It'll be four days before I get my bonus and can replace that money! Don't ever tell me again not to be a jobber-nowl and a mooncalf!*

EGBERT holding up his hand : *Don't worry — leave everything to me.*

OG : *That's just what caused this!*

As he scuttles away, OG looks after him. It is quite obvious that whatever EGBERT's counsel, he is going to do a little plain and fancy worrying. As he looks at JOHNSON's card again . . .

The card is now being held in different fingers. Camera pulls back to disclose that MYRTLE has it. OG is with her.[59]

They are sitting on the porch of the SOUSE home, with OG looking even more depressed than before. MYRTLE is asking :

MYRTLE : *But what about this Mr J. George Johnson?*

OG : *He just means that our engagement's off, that's all.*

MYRTLE : *Og!*

OG : *Well, then, only off for a while if you're willing to wait until I get out of prison.*

MYRTLE : *Og, stop fooling! What do you mean?*

OG : *Your father brought a man into the bank this morning who sold me his old grandmother's paisley shawl with beer running through it or something.*

MYRTLE : *Are you sick?*

OG : *Sure am. Your father got me to take seven hundred dollars from the bank funds and invest it . . .*

MYRTLE : *Oh, Og!*

OG : *But everybody knows beefsteak doesn't come from a mine!*

MYRTLE : *Oh, has he got you drinking too?*

OG : *Might just as well have been. Bewitched me or something, I guess — got me to thinking how I oughta have more money before we got married — so we could have a nice place, and all . . .*

MYRTLE : *Nice place! I'd live in a tent — if it was my own tent! Oh, why does he always have to interfere!*

OG : *Maybe it'll work out. He said not to worry — to leave everything to him.*

MYRTLE suddenly : *So that's what he meant!*[60]

As OG looks at her, she goes on quickly.

MYRTLE continuing : *He told me the same thing just before you got here. He was on his way downtown — said not to worry — just to leave everything to him.*

OG slowly : *Say — you don't suppose he's doing anything desper-*

169

ate, do you?

Near Black Pussy Cat Café. EGBERT and JOHNSON are walking along, on the best of terms.

JOHNSON: *I must say, it was mighty nice of you to call me, Mr Sousé.*

EGBERT: *Oh, not at all — not at all. You're a stranger here, and my business is to make a stranger's stay more pleasant. I work for the Chamber of Commerce when not on my regular job at the bank. Lompoc is noted for its pretty girls; perhaps you've noticed them?*

JOHNSON bashfully: *Ah, yes I have, but I'm a married man with a grown daughter eighteen years of age.*

EGBERT: *Mm! I'd like to meet her . . .* catching himself *. . . I'm very fond of children. I've a grown daughter about to marry. I also have a young daughter, a nice wife and a mother-in-law that loves me like her own son — sometimes even more so.*

JOHNSON pleasantly: *I can well understand that, Mr Sousé.*

EGBERT halts, looks up.[61]

They have reached the Black Pussy Cat Café.

EGBERT: *Ah — the Snack Bar! Do you ever take a little libation?*

JOHNSON: *Well, I seldom drink — but perhaps for sociability's sake . . .*

EGBERT: *That's as good a reason as any!*

They enter the café, taking seats at table in booth.[62]

EGBERT: *What's your pleasure?*

JOHNSON as JOE enters scene: *A rye highball with plenty of soda — make it light.*

EGBERT to JOE: *Hello, Cowboy — how're they treating you?*

JOE: *Okay.*

EGBERT following JOE to bar: *A rye highball and poultice. And by the way, has Michael Finn been in this afternoon?*

JOE glancing at JOHNSON: *No, but he will be.*

EGBERT: *How did Gumlegs come out in the fourth today?*

JOE: *It was a six horse race. He ran seventh!*

EGBERT exits from scene.

EGBERT to JOHNSON: *I saw him run first once, but the jockey had to get off at the three-quarter post and carry him past the tape on his back. He's a beetle.*[63]

JOE is behind the bar, mixing drinks. He produces a little

170

package from his vest pocket, breaks seal and dumps the powder into one of the highballs. He cuts a slice of lemon, marks the glass by sticking the lemon on rim. He picks up tray.

EGBERT and JOHNSON are together in booth.

EGBERT : *Well, down the hatch.*

He tosses off the drink. MR JOHNSON follows suit, but more slowly.

EGBERT : *Tell me, Mr Johnson, how did you happen to become addicted to rye highballs?*

JOHNSON looking suddenly a little queezy : *I'm not addicted . . .*

EGBERT : *I would say you look a little addicted — Personally, they do the strangest things to me. Don't they to you?*

JOHNSON is doing his best to appear polite; he tries to control himself.

JOHNSON : *Well, yes — to tell the truth, I do feel a little peculiar.*

EGBERT : *Peculiar? They make me downright sick!*

JOHNSON increasingly affected : *I'm afraid they have the same effect on me.*

EGBERT : *Yes, sir — they almost kill me. Don't they you?*

JOHNSON : *Why — yes, they do! I've never had such a feeling as this in all my life . . .*

EGBERT : *Are you sure you haven't been eating something lately?*

JOHNSON : *I don't know — but come, let's get out of here — quickly!*[64]

He starts out, EGBERT with him, grasping his arm.

EGBERT and JOHNSON go to door.

EGBERT : *Probably that's what it is then — you haven't been eating properly — or drinking the right things. Or it might be the altitude. This town is five hundred feet above sea level . . . has a population of fifteen hundred . . .*

EGBERT and JOHNSON emerging from the saloon.

EGBERT continuing : *. . . schools, churches, public library — six blocks of paved streets — four trains a day . . .* They start up sidewalk *. . . not counting the milk train that goes through at four o'clock in the morning — three drug stores — one of them sells medicine . . .*

JOHNSON halting : *Stop — stop — I'm dying — take me to a culvert.*

171

EGBERT: *Why don't you wait until you get to the hotel? It's only six blocks.*

They start out of scene.

JOHNSON: *My poor wife!*

EGBERT holding him up: *How would you like a nice bowl of chili? Maybe that would help.*[65]

JOHNSON groans.

EGBERT half-carrying, half-dragging JOHNSON into hotel lobby. CLERK at desk. EGBERT and JOHNSON entering. EGBERT pilots JOHNSON towards desk.

The CLERK confronts EGBERT and JOHNSON.

CLERK: *If your friend is drunk, don't bring him into this hotel!*

EGBERT: *He's already registered here. He has ptomaine poisoning or something. His name is Johnson. J. George Johnson.*

CLERK: *Well, get him out of sight as quickly as possible.*

CLERK bows to snooty-looking woman who enters scene, stares at JOHNSON and EGBERT with disgust.

CLERK to EGBERT: *He's in room three.*[66]

As EGBERT takes JOHNSON away the LADY looks dubious.

The LADY remains with the CLERK.

LADY: *I thought this was a family hotel.*

CLERK: *Indeed it is — Mr Johnson got a touch of ptomaine at a family picnic.*

He hands her the pen with a flourish. She takes it dubiously, still uncertain.

LADY: *Well, I don't know . . .*

She is just about to sign, when there is a sound off. As they turn . . .

. . . EGBERT carries a man into the lobby. This is too much for the LADY. She turns and drops the pen and starts out.

LADY: *Family hotel? What kind of family?*

The CLERK is staring. He comes out from behind the desk. He joins the group at the desk.

CLERK: *What are you trying to do — fill this hotel with a lot of Delirium Tremens? We've a reputation to uphold.*

EGBERT: *It's the same man. He just fell out of the window.*

CLERK: *Well, get him up to his room — quickly!*

EGBERT: *Look, my friend, it's your hotel — if you want him out*

172

of the way, you take him up!

The CLERK gives a snort of impatience and starts to assist JOHNSON.

CLERK: *Come, Mr. Johnson, let's pull ourselves together.*

EGBERT: *You sound just like the coach of the crew. Rowed myself, once . . . Carlisle School for Indians, class of . . .* He passes his hand over his mouth to pass over the date . . . *Good coach we had too — old Bus McCarey — used to feed us steaming hot pork sandwiches garnished with codfish gravy.*

As the CLERK leads JOHNSON away, a hollow moan floats back. EGBERT looks after him shaking his head.

EGBERT: *No stamina — no stamina.*

As he speaks he has picked up the telephone on the desk.[67]

As EGBERT picks up phone, he reacts to VOICE coming from it.

VOICE: *When you hear the tone it will be twenty-two and one-half minutes 'til seven.*

EGBERT: *I'm calling Doctor Stall . . .* looks at watch . . . *and another thing, it will not be twenty-two and a half minutes 'til seven . . . it will be twenty-two and a half minutes 'til six.*

VOICE: *Excuse, please.*

He jiggles phone. VOICE answers.

VOICE: *Hello-ah. I'll give you information please-ah.*

EGBERT: *See here! — This is no time for radio programs! I want Dr Stall!*

VOICE: *Louder, please.*

EGBERT very loud: *Dr Stall! What do you mean speak louder? . . .* He mumbles . . . *If I spoke any louder I wouldn't need a phone.*[68]

We are in DR STALL's office. There is an undersized, emaciated-looking man with a drooping mustache standing before the DOCTOR's desk. He is naked from the waist up, his hands are hanging down by his side, his suspenders are also hanging. His ribs are plainly visible. The DOCTOR is talking on telephone.

DOCTOR STALL into phone: *Just a moment, please . . .* fairly feminine; to the man before his desk, very masculine . . . *The first thing you've got to do is cut out all health foods for a while . . . pardon me . . .* into telephone, feminine, *Hello . . . hello . . . Dr Stall speaking . . .* looks over at the patient and in a rather stern, business-like voice, says, *That will be ten dollars, please. The nurse will return your clothes with the receipt* . . . into phone — feminine voice, *Hello* . . . *sorry to keep you waiting. Who is speaking* . . . ?

Close shot of EGBERT at phone.

EGBERT into phone: *Listen, Doc — there's an ol' friend of the family here at the hotel. He's evidently been on a bender* . . . *drinking too much.*

DR STALL'S VOICE: *I see.*[69]

EGBERT: *His wife wired me this morning — said when he gets on a bender you got to keep him in bed four or five days. Can you come over and give him the mumbo-jumbo?* . . . *Okay, fine.*

As he hangs up, the CLERK enters the shot, happy but . . .

. . . He then sees EGBERT.

CLERK: *Say — he's heavy.*

EGBERT lightly: *Oh, that's because he's got an extra fin.*

As the CLERK looks at him puzzled, he goes on quickly.

EGBERT continuing: *Doc Stall is on his way over — send him right up. Meanwhile I'll see Johnson doesn't lean out the window too far.*

He starts toward the stairs.

Inside JOHNSON's hotel room: JOHNSON is in bed, groaning and with a deadly pallor on his face. EGBERT enters.[70]

EGBERT: *Hello, baby. How do you feel now?*

JOHNSON groaning: *I feel as though I've been poisoned.*

EGBERT: *I can't believe it. Why you look the veritable picture of health.*

JOHNSON sits up in bed, leaning forward to catch a reflection of his face in the mirror of a dressing table.

EGBERT: *If you looked any healthier you'd crack the mirror! How about a little snack?*

JOHNSON presses one hand quickly over his mouth, with the other he beckons EGBERT to go away from him.

EGBERT: *Why don't you let me order you some nice hot milk and some breaded veal cutlet with tomato sauce?*

With an agonized look at EGBERT, JOHNSON jumps out of bed and rushes to the bathroom. EGBERT calls out:

EGBERT: *And a nice chocolate eclair and with whipped camembert.*

From the bathroom we hear JOHNSON's groans.

174

JOHNSON'S VOICE: *Go away, please . . .*

There is a knock on the door and DR STALL enters as JOHNSON comes out of the bathroom and crawls into bed.

EGBERT: *This is the eminent Dr Stall, our town's leading physician and diagnostician. Tell him just how you feel. Tell him everything. Tell him what you did to Philadelphia Jack O'Brien. He's a doctor. Everything is confidential.*

EGBERT is on one side of the bed, DR STALL on the other. JOHNSON is lying stricken between him.

DOCTOR taking his record book and pencil from his pocket: *What is the name?*

JOHNSON weakly: *J. George Johnson.*

DOCTOR: *Your business?*

JOHNSON: *Bank examiner.*

DOCTOR: *Bank examiner? A rather lucrative occupation. Do you mind showing me your tongue?*

JOHNSON sticks out his tongue belligerently.

DOCTOR looking at it: *Hmmmmm — You've got to eat more solids — meats and sauces. You need iron, liver and bacon. You lack vitamins A. B. and C. — skip the rest down to X. Y. — if Z. is necessary, we can give you that later. First of all you need rest — rest will do you more good than all the doctors in the world. No exercise.*

DOCTOR STALL bends over, picks up his black bag from the floor, places it on bed, opens it and takes from it a jar about the size of a glass pickle jar. It is filled with ping-pong balls.[71]

DOCTOR: *Take two of these in a glass of caster oil two nights running, then skip one night.*

JOHNSON weakly: *But I thought you told me not to take any exercise.*

DOCTOR: *You take me too literally. I should have said — two nights consecutively and then jump one night.*

JOHNSON: *Jump?*

DOCTOR: *Er — refrain from taking them. With proper rest, I shall have you out of here in three days . . .*

EGBERT looks at DOCTOR: *Three days . . . ?*

EGBERT puts four fingers up to the DOCTOR, reminding him that it will be four days before the second, when OG gets his bonus from the bank. The DOCTOR doesn't get the signal,

175

and continues:

DOCTOR: *Yes, I'll have you out in three days.*

EGBERT stomps his cane four times upon the floor, signalling the DOCTOR again that it will require four days for OG to get his bonus. The DOCTOR doesn't get it. EGBERT uses his cane as a golf club and says, as he swings his cane:

EGBERT: *Fore!*[72]

DOCTOR still oblivious: *Be careful waving your cane like that. You might break something.*

EGBERT: *Three days . . . that will be the day before the boys at the bank get their bonuses.*

DOCTOR: *Yes, I'll have you out in three days . . . unless, of course, complications set in — and then it will naturally take another day.*

EGBERT: *Well, Doc, we'd better get going . . .* He wipes his brow, then turns to JOHNSON *. . . If you need anything, don't fail to call on me.*

JOHNSON: *Go — go — go!* He waves his hand frantically.

EGBERT and the DOCTOR exit.

On his way home, EGBERT passes the Lompoc Savoy Ritz, the local movie emporium. From the marquee, the owner is taking down a sign which reads: " Bank Night Tonite — $2,500." EGBERT hails the impresario.

EGBERT: *Ah there, Mr Harriman — tonight was the night of the super-colossal prize, wasn't it?*

HARRIMAN disappointed in him: *It isn't like you to forget, Mr Sousé. How'd it happen?*

EGBERT: *Oh, an appointment. You know, large affairs, big business — a conference with Mr George Johnson and Mr Mickey Finn. By the way, who won?*

HARRIMAN: *You did.*

EGBERT: *I drew — the twenty-five hundred dollar prize?*

As EGBERT digs into his vest pocket for end of ticket stubs, MR HARRIMAN nods sadly.

HARRIMAN: *Yeh — too bad you weren't here to claim it. Had to draw again. Mr Skinner, president of the Lompoc National, was the lucky man the second time.*

EGBERT crushed: *Oh yes, Mr Skinner — and him with a whole bank full of lettuce.*

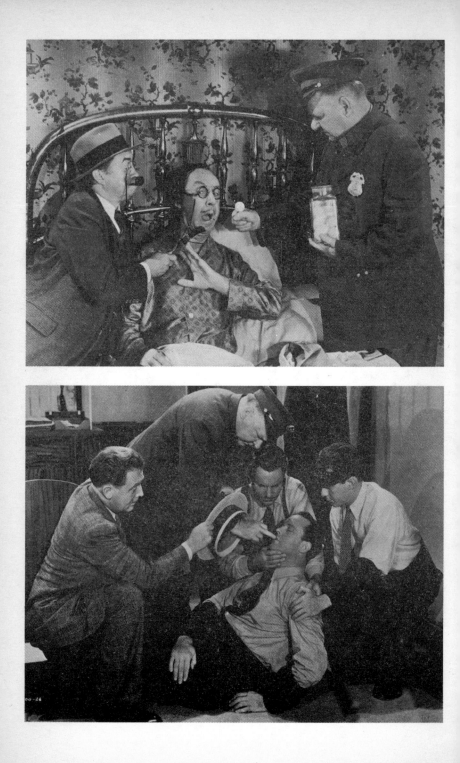

HARRIMAN: *Too bad you were so busy — but you got the consolation award anyhow.*

From a box beside the theatre entrance he lifts a package.

HARRIMAN: *This fine set of flower-patterned dishes, service for six.*

EGBERT still stunned, he nods: *Flower pattern — service for six — and I could have won the twenty-five hundred fish?*

HARRIMAN nods again: *I'm sorry, Mr Sousé — but you know the rules. However...*

EGBERT: *Yeh — however, I got the consolation prize.*

HARRIMAN: *Make a mighty fine wedding present for your daughter when she marries young Oggilby... G'night.*

EGBERT starts on his way again. The irony of MR HARRIMAN's words is the crowning touch. If he'd only not been so busy trying to out-manoeuvre MR JOHNSON, everything now would be all right. He answers weakly:

EGBERT: *Good night...*

It is night, as EGBERT comes up the walk carrying the dishes he sees MYRTLE sitting on the porch steps. He speaks with a forced jauntiness:

EGBERT: *Hello, Myrtle. You see me out — you see me in!*

MYRTLE ominously: *I was waiting for you.*

EGBERT: *And mighty glad you're going to be that you did!*

He holds up the bundle of dishes.

EGBERT continuing: *The first present for your own little nest — a set of deluxe crockery.*

As MYRTLE doesn't say anything, he goes on somewhat forcedly:

EGBERT continuing: *Of course, it isn't twenty-five hundred smacks — that would have been a present! But it ain't exactly a kick in the shins, either.*

MYRTLE: *I've had my kick in the shins ... Og investigated this afternoon — and there isn't any Beefsteak Mine.*

EGBERT: *No...! Oh, say now — there must be a mistake!*

MYRTLE: *Yes, and you made it. Oh Dad, why did you have to interfere? Now I'll probably never get married!*

EGBERT: *Gosh, if I'd only gone to the movies instead of Mickey Finning.*

MYRTLE bursting out: *That all you think about — a good time!*

Oh, it's easy for you not to care. You'll just pull out and go fish-ing, or to a billiard tournament, or something. But I'll be stuck here — forever — and it'll all be your fault!

MYRTLE now is nearly hysterical and she courses on:

MYRTLE continuing: *And you can keep your old dishes — because there won't be any wedding!*

With this she turns and runs into the house.

EGBERT stands looking after Myrtle, realizing what he has done to her happiness.[73]

EGBERT enters briskly, and starts across the floor. Again he greets people, with small response.

EGBERT is making his salutes.

EGBERT: *Good morning ... good morning ...*

No one pays any attention to him. EGBERT moves on towards OG's cage.

EGBERT comes over to OG.

EGBERT: *Good morning, Og.*

OG wearily: *Hello, Mr Sousé.*

EGBERT: *Now, now, my boy — stiff upper lip. Everything is fine and dandy. Our friend Johnson is bedded with a sharp case of sea sickness.*

OG happily: *Do you think he'll stay away until I'm able to put that seven hundred back? I don't get my bonus for four days, remember.*

EGBERT airily: *I remember. And Johnson will stay in bed if I have to Finn-ize him again.*

With this, he moves on about his duties,[74] as he sees them, of being sort of a greeter for the bank. Camera pans with him as he crosses the lobby bidding customers good morning, and asking them if there is anything he can do for them. Despite his good will, no one pays much attention to him. We look towards SKINNER's door. SKINNER is standing in the doorway, beckoning to EGBERT. He goes inside and EGBERT follows.

Inside SKINNER's office: STENOGRAPHER ready for dictation, book in her hand, her legs still crossed. EGBERT enters. Again EGBERT, while SKINNER is talking to him, does by-play with STENOGRAPHER — unable to resist the lure of her legs.[75]

SKINNER to EGBERT indignantly : *Mr Sousé, we appreciate the capture you made the other day — and the manhandling you gave those criminals . . .*

EGBERT : *Well, it wasn't so bad, considering the size of the knife he pulled on me. Honest, it was this long . . .*

He holds out both arms full length — finds that's not long enough — measures a distance from end of desk to wall.

EGBERT continuing : *. . . from here to over there.*

SKINNER : *Doesn't anybody ever pull a short knife on you, Mr Sousé?* . . . He holds up his hands about six inches apart . . . *a little one about that long?*

EGBERT : *A midget did once — a little colored midget, Major Moe — Now that I come to think of it, it was a razor he pulled. No — the blade of a safety razor.*

SKINNER giving him a look : *To continue — we're grateful to you for retrieving the bank's funds, and we think we've shown our gratitude by giving you a position here. But, when you caution Mrs Muckle's little son about carrying a toy pistol into the bank, that's carrying caution too far.*[76]

EGBERT : *Oh, Mr Skinner, that's where you're wrong! Caution can't be carried too far. Why, I remember that self-same midget — Major Moe — pulled a little automatic on me — and I thought it was a toy . . . Well, needless to say . . .*

SKINNER interrupting : *I also have been informed that you are a frequenter of a café known as the Black Pussy. Take warning, Mr Sousé.*

EGBERT : *I can explain everything. You see . . .*

SKINNER : *Never mind . . . thank you . . .*

EGBERT : *Thank you, Mr Skinner.*

With a flourish, he turns to the STENOGRAPHER and hands her a napkin ring.

EGBERT : *Will you accept this silver-plated napkin ring with my compliments? I won it in a recent joust at the bowling alley.*

STENOGRAPHER accepting it : *Thank you.*

As he turns his back, she drops it into the wastebasket. This action is almost simultaneous with the entrance of J. GEORGE JOHNSON, the bank examiner. He carries a light portfolio and a heavy load of woe. EGBERT stares at him, thunderstruck.[77]

SKINNER : *Why, Mr Johnson!*

183

Camera pans him quickly over to JOHNSON, his hand out-stretched. EGBERT is in the background.

JOHNSON is greeted by SKINNER.

SKINNER: *It's an unexpected pleasure to see you in Lompoc.*

JOHNSON: *No pleasure for me. I'm a sick man, Mr Skinner. But I'm also a man for duty. If you don't mind, I'd like to go over your books.*

SKINNER with banker heartiness: *Why, of course we don't mind! The Lompoc National is always ready for an audit, yes siree!*

EGBERT weakly, from the background: *Yes siree . . .*[78]

SKINNER indicates him to JOHNSON.

SKINNER, JOHNSON and EGBERT together.

SKINNER: *Mr Sousé, our special officer here, will give you any assistance you wish. Mr Johnson is the bank examiner, Mr Sousé.*

EGBERT: *Yes, I know . . .*

SKINNER: *Not feeling well, you say, Mr Johnson?*

JOHNSON a little grimly: *Mr Sousé knows that too.*

SKINNER: *Oh, so you gentlemen already are acquainted. Fine — fine! Then I'll just leave you to Mr Sousé, and rest assured that you're in proper hands.*

He bows and clicks his heels again. EGBERT does the same and takes JOHNSON's arm.

EGBERT: *This way, Mr Johnson. And you're sure you've had your breakfast?*

JOHNSON gives a low moan and goes out with him.[79]

An empty cage containing a desk and stool: JOHNSON enters, followed by EGBERT, who carries two big ledgers. The adjoining cage is OG's.

EGBERT: *Here are the tellers' books, Mr Johnson — now you just go ahead and add 'em up to your heart's content . . . By the way, you're sure you don't want a sandwich?*

JOHNSON waving aside the suggestion: *There are only two ledgers here, Mr Sousé — where's the third?*

EGBERT: *The third?*

JOHNSON has looked into OG's section — sees the ledger. He holds out his hand and speaks to OG.[80]

JOHNSON: *Teller, would you mind giving me your ledger for an audit? I'll balance your cash against it later.*

OG dismally: *Certainly.*

184

He hands it over, giving EGBERT a forlorn look. EGBERT reaches at the ledger.

EGBERT: *Let me help you, Mr Johnson. I'll check this one over. Very good at it, really . . .*

JOHNSON icily: *Thank you, but I prefer to do it myself.*

He opens the ledger. EGBERT plugs in the electric fan.

EGBERT: *Pretty warm today, isn't it?*

The leaves of the ledger begin to flutter. JOHNSON clutches at them wildly.

JOHNSON: *Turn that thing off!*

EGBERT: *But isn't it hot in here?*

JOHNSON: *Hot? I've a chill!*

He reaches over and pulls the plug. EGBERT grabs up a large ink bottle.

EGBERT: *How about some nice fresh ink?*

He stumbles purposefully and splashes ink toward the ledger. JOHNSON snatches it to safety just in time.

JOHNSON: *For heaven's sake, man? Will you please go away and let me get my work done!*

EGBERT regretfully: *Nothing else I can do for you?*

JOHNSON: *You've done plenty as it is!*

EGBERT glumly: *Yes, I guess I have.*

He backs sadly out.

EGBERT continuing: *Can't I run out and get you a nice cup of hot fish?*

JOHNSON: *Go away — go away!*

EGBERT: *Well, all right. I was only trying to be helpful.*

He looks at OG as he says this, and lifts his hands in a shrug. As he turns away.

OG looks mighty unhappy. He sees JOHNSON open his ledger and sighs:

OG: *The hour of judgement certainly is coming up!*[81]

EGBERT comes out from behind the cage and approaches a customer writing out a check at one of the small desks.

EGBERT comes to the man, still trying to be business-like.

EGBERT: *A good, good morning Mr . . . and is there anything I can do for you?*

MAN: *Yes.*

The man turns around — and reveals himself to be the bandit

who escaped yesterday. EGBERT's eyes pop as he sees the gun levelled at him. EGBERT starts to turn.

EGBERT: *Excuse me. This is where I came in.*

CROOK: *Just a minute . . . there is something you can do for me . . . be my bodyguard . . . Turn around.*

EGBERT turns around, as he seeks to explain.

EGBERT: *Really, it was all an accident . . . I was just sitting there on the bus bench pursuing my education . . . never had the chance to go to college y'know.*

CROOK: *I don't know and don't care! Now start walking over to that cashier's cage — and this time there won't be any chump in the way — except you!*

EGBERT and the CROOK cross the foyer. The CROOK's gun is beneath EGBERT's arm.

EGBERT: *Er . . . somebody got in your way last time?*

CROOK: *Yes, and would I like to get my hands on him!*

EGBERT anxiously: *Oh, I daresay he's a very nice fellow . . .*

CROOK: *He'll be a very dead fellow if he gets in front of me again!*

EGBERT weakly: *I daresay.*

They now have come up to OG's cage.

Close shot at OG's cage: as the bandit, using EGBERT as protection, comes up to OG he tosses a small hand-satchel on the counter and says, tersely:

CROOK: *I'm back again — it's a stick-up!*

OG stares at the two. EGBERT says, uneasily:

EGBERT: *You remember him, don't you, Og?*

OG stunned: *Yeh! I do.*

CROOK: *Then you know what I want . . . so toss it over.*

As he wiggles the gun meaningly, OG hastily begins to put money in the satchel.

OG: *Yes, sir . . .*

EGBERT seeing a chance: *Put in an extra seven hundred, Oggie boy.*

As OG looks at him in surprise EGBERT winks.[82]

EGBERT: *What's seven hundred more or less at a time like this?*

CROOK: *Say, you're all right!*

EGBERT: *Nothing at all . . . nothing at all. Just courtesy of the house.*

The CROOK grabs up the satchel.

CROOK: *Okay, then — you can show me to the door.*

As they turn to go, in the same lock step, EGBERT indicates the satchel with his head and says to OG:

EGBERT: *All that — and seven hundred too!*

CROOK: *Just a minute — I want to give him a receipt . . .*

He leans over and conks OG with his pistol butt. OG disappears.

CROOK continuing: *Just to make sure he stays off that alarm, this time . . . All right, let's go.*

EGBERT indicates JOHNSON in the next booth and says under his breath:

EGBERT: *You don't think he might step on it, do you?*

CROOK: *Say, you are all right — better take no chances.*

He leans over and raps JOHNSON to sleep, then says to EGBERT:

CROOK: *That'll take care of him.*

EGBERT: *I hope so!*

The two march across the foyer, a couple of customers look at them, but otherwise they march along unmolested to the door and through it.

As the CROOK bundles EGBERT through the door, they almost collide with MARTIN DODDS.

DODDS: *Hello, Mr Sousé — I've been looking for you.*

EGBERT: *Hello, Mr Dodds — been making any gangster movies lately?*

CROOK breaking in: *Sousé! Then it was you — why sure it was — how could I forget a puss like that! — Come on — I'm taking you with me!*

As he speaks, quickly and savagely, he jerks the gun out from beneath EGBERT's arm and menaces both men with it.[88]

CROOK: *Get out of the way, and you won't get hurt — Get in that car, you!*

He indicates the little old LADY's car.

It is still standing at the curb, where we saw it last. But now both the LADY and the CHAUFFEUR are gone, and a " For Sale " sign hangs on it. As he bustles EGBERT toward it the alarm siren in the bank begins to sound.

CROOK: *Get in the back seat, dope — you're the bullet screen!*

EGBERT alarmed: *The bullet — hey!*

But it is too late. The CROOK has jumped into the front seat and started the car off with a loud roar. As it careers away.[84] Patrons and employees run out of the bank crying "Hold-up!" "Right in front of me!" "Call the police!" etc. OG is in the foreground.

OG : *He took Mr Sousé!*

DODDS : *He certainly did — right from under my contract!*

SKINNER comes running in.

SKINNER : *I called the police . . . Hello, Mr Dodds . . which way did they go?*

DODDS : *That way — come on! I've got a car!*

As they race toward where it stands and start to get in, the police car pulls up. SKINNER directs it excitedly.

SKINNER : *That way! Hold-up — bandits!*

DODDS has started his car with a lurch. As the two cars race off down the street . . .

The chase is engaged in by the three cars — the first containing EGBERT and the bank robber; the second, two policemen; and the third, DODDS, OG and SKINNER. As the cars race along country roads with squealing tyres, around hairpin turns, intercut with close shots of the various cars.

EGBERT and the CROOK : The CROOK is driving, furiously, with EGBERT in the back seat as his protection. Despite the terrific pace at which they are moving, EGBERT at all times retains his dignity, and when he moves, even to dodge bullets, it is at his usual deliberate tempo, muttering irritably. He is not even unduly affected when a litter of bullets tattoos the crown of his hat.

The police car contains the two upholders of the law. During this flash they speak.

FIRST COP : *You know who's driving that car — Mopey Murphy!*

SECOND COP : *Say — there's a five thousand dollar dead-or-alive reward on him!*

FIRST COP reaching for his gun : *Get out your gun!*

DODDS, OG and SKINNER are all in the front seat of DODD's car. When the sound of the COPS shooting begins to come over, OG quavers.

OG : *They're liable to hit Mr Sousé!*

188

DODDS : *And me with ten thousand in my pocket for him!*
SKINNER : *For Sousé — what for?*
DODDS : *A story he told yesterday when he was directing. I sent it in with the day's report — and the boss went nuts about it. Wants it and Sousé too.*
OG wailing : *Oh, if Mr Sousé only knew!*

EGBERT is in the bandit car, dodging bullets. He speaks uneasily to MURPHY.
EGBERT : *Don't you think we'd better stop? The law always wins, y'know.*
CROOK grimly : *Not this time it won't — even if you get shot a dozen times.*
EGBERT : *I'll settle for less.*

The motor suddenly begins to knock. The others are gaining.
CROOK : *Great grief — what's that?*
EGBERT : *It's this car — I know it well.*
CROOK : *We gotta get off the road!*

He wheels the car off the road onto a dirt road. The other two cars race past the turn-off.
A SIGN :

TO LAKE TALAHASEE

NICODEMUS is sitting on a small tree, above the " Lake Tala-hasee " sign, where we saw him last. He looks off and croaks :
NICODEMUS : *Well, well, look who's here!*

The car carrying EGBERT and MURPHY limps into the shot.
NICODEMUS : *The suckers must be biting again!*[85]

MURPHY jumps out of the car, flourishing his pistol at EGBERT.
MURPHY : *Come on, you said you knew the car. Now fix it!*
EGBERT : *Easily said, my friend — not so easily accomplished. I am strictly the kind of mechanic who needs the tools of his trade. Have you a shifting spanner?*

MURPHY grabs a kit off the seat beside him.
MURPHY : *Here's the best set of burglar tools in my trade. See if you can find a whatever-it-is in there.*

EGBERT opens the bag. He talks as he does so.
EGBERT : *Handy little kit you have here, Mr . . . complete for all occasions — opening nights and such.*

He picks up a small vial of colorless fluid.

189

EGBERT continuing: *Looks like a little medicine got mixed in by mistake.*

MURPHY: *Hey, that's explosive!*

But it is too late. EGBERT has nonchalantly tossed it to one side. There is an immediate GREAT EXPLOSION.

We see the police car as the BOOM comes over.

FIRST COP: *What was that?*

SECOND COP: *It might mean Murphy!*

He starts to turn the car.

EGBERT and MURPHY pick themselves up from the ground. Both are stripped to their underwear. EGBERT is wearing a brave red flannel ensemble.

EGBERT: *You must be a very sick man to use stuff that strong!*

NICODEMUS' VOICE: *Hey . . . !*

NICODEMUS is in the tree, which is denuded of all its leaves just as NICODEMUS (a fake, I hasten to say) is minus all his feathers. NICODEMUS is sore. He squawks:

NICODEMUS: *. . . you can't do this to me!*[86]

MURPHY is very angry too.

MURPHY: *You blundering idiot. You trying to kill me?*

EGBERT: *Well, it's an idea.*

He eyes MURPHY's underpants, which are pretty fancy.

EGBERT: *Tailored by Schiaparelli, I presume?*

MURPHY waving his gun as he grates: *Oh, if only I knew how to fix a car!*

EGBERT says with a lofty sneer:

EGBERT: *We learned such things at my reform school.*

MURPHY is rapidly losing his small fund of patience. He flourishes the gun again.

MURPHY: *Come on you, take your choice — get busy or get dead!*

EGBERT: *Now don't get hasty — even you should know a mechanic can't do anything without a helper.*

MURPHY: *All right! All right! What'll I do . . . ?*

EGBERT: *Just get underneath and give me a hand with the snorf.*

MURPHY getting under the car: *The what?*

EGBERT: *Underneath — that gadget with the nebbish.*

MURPHY: *Which one?*

EGBERT: *You'll find out.*

He gives the nut a twist that he turned yesterday and once

more the engine falls out of the car. This time it pins the hapless MURPHY beneath it. MURPHY screams.[87]

MURPHY : *Hey — what'er you doing? I'm caught!*

EGBERT lightly : *I'm afraid you are, my larcenous friend.*

He saunters away.

NICODEMUS sourly : *Wise guy.*

Into the scene races the police car. EGBERT comes to it gracefully.

EGBERT : *Looking for someone?*

FIRST COP climbing out of car : *Where is he?*

EGBERT : *Where is who — whom?*

SECOND COP : *The thief — Murphy!*

EGBERT : *Oh him . . .* indicates off *. . . he's over there.*

MURPHY squeals again. The COP pulls his gun and signals to the other COP to follow.

COP : *Careful, he's dangerous.*

EGBERT easily : *Not at all. It's quite safe. I've taken care of him.*

As the COPS go for MURPHY, the car driven by DODDS pulls up. OG leaps out first and comes to EGBERT.

OG : *Are you hurt, Mr Sousé?*

EGBERT : *Nothing at all, Og my boy. Things looked shaky when he pulled that ghurka sword on me — but I subdued him. Power of mine, perhaps . . .* sotto voce he says quickly *. . . Remember, he stole seven hundred[88] more'n they'll find.*

DODDS enters the shot.

DODDS joining them : *This seems to be your day, Mr Sousé . . .*

EGBERT : *Nothing at all — nothing at all — just in the line of duty.*[89]

The COPS now have MURPHY manacled. As they lead him to their car, one holds up the satchel.

FIRST COP : *Got it again.*

SECOND COP : *Better drop by the station and see about your reward, Mr Sousé.*

EGBERT : *Reward?*

SECOND COP : *Sure — there's a five thousand dollar prize for this muzzler.*

They take him away.

EGBERT reacts to the good news.

EGBERT : *A jack pot!*

Egbert with the rest of group.

Og : *Say, it sure is your day — Pop!*

Egbert with a deprecatory shrug : *Nothing more than the beneficent effects of correct living.*

Dodds : *And correct thinking . . .*

He opens his wallet and takes out a check.

Dodds : *Here's ten thousand from the Tel-Aviz company for that story you told yesterday. As well as a contract for you to bring it to the screen.*

Egbert uncomfortably : *You mean a — job?*

Nicodemus warningly : *Careful, Egbert.*

Dodds : *Why, yes — directing like you used to do.*

Egbert still uncomfortable : *Ah, yes — in the good old days.*

Nicodemus relentlessly : *You've got fifteen grand, Egbert — don't be a pig.*

Egbert heeding his advice : *Give the job to a more needy man, Mr Dodds. The money I will accept and put to good use . . .* he looks at Og, who grins . . . *especially seven hundred dollars of it.*

Egbert grins in anticipation.

Egbert : *And I imagine the rest of the bundle will do a little something for me!*

Close shot of a breakfast table, richly appointed and loaded with a complete breakfast. Egbert is revealed just putting down his coffee cup. On his face is the arrogant yet benign expression of a master in his own house. Elsie Mae comes running in with a newspaper.[90]

Elsie Mae : *Here's the morning paper, papa dear.*

Egbert accepting with dignity : *Thank you, my child — now run upstairs and get me a suitable cigar from the handsome humidor on my new dresser.*

Elsie Mae : *Yes, papa dear.*

As she scampers off, Agatha Souse comes from the kitchen with a coffee urn.

Agatha : *Here's some fresh coffee, Egbert dear.*

Egbert here opens the paper. He smiles broadly.

Egbert : *Ah ha!*

Agatha : *Good news, darling?*

Egbert : *Good enough.*

He shows her the newspaper.

Shot of LOMPOC BEAGLE which features linked photographs of MYRTLE and OG, labelled " Mr and Mrs Oglethorpe Oggilby." There is a caption :

NEWLYWEDS TO NIAGARA FALLS

We go back to

AGATHA : *Myrtle married — isn't it wonderful? Egbert, is it true that married people live longer?*

EGBERT rising : *No, it just seems longer.*

He starts across the room. When he reaches the kitchen door he knocks on it briskly.

The door opens and MRS BRUNCH, wearing a kitchen apron, looks out. EGBERT gives her a condescending nod.

EGBERT : *A very nice breakfast, Mrs Brunch.*

MRS BRUNCH : *Oh, thank you, Egbert — I'm so glad you enjoyed it.*

He bows in dignified fashion and goes on.

As he picks up his hat, near the front door, ELSIE MAE comes down with the cigar.

ELSIE MAE : *Here you are, popsie-wopsie.*

EGBERT : *Thank you, my little chickadee. And don't get so familiar.*

He takes the cigar, settles his hat, and raps her smartly on the skull. As AGATHA enters the shot she says :

AGATHA : *Hurry home when you feel like it, Egbert dear. I'll wait up for you.*

EGBERT : *If there are any important calls for me, I'll be at the office.*

He nods pleasantly to his wife and daughter.

EGBERT : *Good morning.*

He goes out.

EGBERT comes along the street. At the curb is a man working on a stalled car. EGBERT pauses and starts to ask if he can be of help.

EGBERT : *What seems to be . . . ?*

Then he checks himself and adds :

EGBERT continuing : *No, I guess not.*

He continues on his way.

EGBERT comes to the door of the Black Pussy Cat and halts.

SIGN :

Out for a drink.
Joe

EGBERT is annoyed, but the logic of the note placates him somewhat.

EGBERT : *Hmmmmm — not a bad idea.*

As he looks thoughtfully off . . .

He sees a pretty girl sitting on the bus bench. She is reading a book — and showing a very nifty expanse of leg.

EGBERT's face clears. He settles his hat and straightens his tie. As, humming jauntily, he starts forward to see if he can win a friend.

THE END

NOTES

1. The opening sequence of the screenplay was abandoned in the actual shooting of the film and a new sequence substituted. We see a street scene in the small town of Lompoc. Automobiles pass up and down the street. Two elegantly dressed ladies walk along a sidewalk by a white paling fence. One of them stops to peer down at a letter box positioned by a gate in the fence. Then we see the letter box in close-up; the words " Egbert Sousé " are printed boldly on it. The two ladies discuss the correct pronunciation of the name.

2. Elsie Mae is reading *Detective* magazine. Throughout this scene there are cuts back and forth from Mrs Brunch to Mrs Souse and Elsie Mae.

3. In the final film version, Myrtle enters at this juncture and exchanges greetings with the assembled family. Mrs Brunch continues delivering her little homily to Mrs Souse. Myrtle suddenly bursts into tears and sobbingly recounts the terrible story of how she has seen her father, Egbert, coming out of a saloon bar, actually smoking a cigarette.

4. This sequence is not in the final version of the film.

5. Egbert enters down the stairs at this point, smoking one of the forbidden cigarettes.

6. Much of the preceding material, from Egbert's entrance onwards, was cut from the final version of the film.

7. This sequence is much amended and expanded in the film. After Egbert has been hit on the head by the bottle, he goes out, then reappears carrying a large jardinière which he makes as if to throw in the direction of Elsie Mae, who promptly ducks beneath the table. Mrs Brunch screams abuse at Egbert. Myrtle prevents Egbert from carrying out his fell intention by rushing to him to introduce him to her financé, Og Oggilby, who we now see standing on the verandah. Egbert chuckles and hands the jardinière to Og, closes the front door of the house and walks away,

coolly raising his hat to MYRTLE and OG.

8. The preceding exchange between EGBERT, OG and MYRTLE was cut from the film version.

9. EGBERT adds a few more annoying comments in the final filmed version, such as, "Are you carrying the proper amount of air in your tyres?" and, "Of course, it may be the wheelbase."

10. The car is in fact an open sedan and the old LADY sits in the back seat.

11. At this point there is a close shot in the film of the CHAUFFEUR's feet firmly stepping on one of EGBERT's.

12. The preceding sequence, from EGBERT's encounter with the old LADY and the CHAUFFEUR, is almost entirely cut from the final film version.

13. DODDS becomes MACKLEY Q. GREENE in the film.

14. These initials become Q.Q. in the film.

15. The above conversation is slightly different in the film version; and at the end of it EGBERT departs, clutching three glasses of liquor.

16. The whole of the preceding sequence concerning OG is cut in the film version.

17. EGBERT tries to break into limping French at this point in the film.

18. FRANCOIS, dressed in tails and topper, looks absurdly shocked at EGBERT's suggestions and exclaims, "In these clothes?" EGBERT coolly replies, "You can change your hat."

19. The following exchange between MISS PLUPP, the SCRIPT GIRL and EGBERT is intercut with scenes of CLAM, very drunk, being walked up and down by two assistants in a quiet corner of the set.

20. The preceding sequence between EGBERT and MISS PLUPP is cut in the film version. Instead, EGBERT sinks back into the directorial rocking-chair and is carried away, palanquin-style, by four assistants.

21. There are a number of additional incidents in the film version at this point. EGBERT sits enthroned in pomp on the directorial chair, issuing directions to FRANCOIS and the starlet. As he is giving orders, he overbalances and crashes over backwards and falls out of his chair and over the edge of the raised platform. A number of assistants rush to help him, but EGBERT flaps churlishly at his would-be helpers.

22. The following exchanges between EGBERT and his family are much more bitter in the film. ELSIE MAE actually demands a part in the film, and when EGBERT starts to rehearse FRANCOIS and the heroine in a romantic scene, she socks him from behind with a megaphone. Then, as EGBERT walks away from the unadmiring members of his family, ELSIE MAE hurls another missile after him and knocks his hat off.

23. CLAM's protests are cut in the film version. At this juncture, EGBERT brusquely hands the script to FRANCOIS and stalks off. DODDS/GREENE glares after him furiously.

24. CLAM protests his fitness to carry on with the film to DODDS/GREENE, then promptly crashes to the ground in a drunken faint again.

25. The preceding exchange between ELSIE MAE, EGBERT and CLAM is cut in the film version.

26. As EGBERT hurries past, the CHAUFFEUR mutters something between his teeth, then is promptly admonished by the old LADY.

27. The preceding sequences, from EGBERT's renewed encounter with the CHAUFFEUR and the old LADY, are cut in the film version.

28. There are slight changes in the order of the robbery sequence in the film version.

29. This sequence begins with EGBERT standing impatiently at the door of The Black Pussy Cat, gazing in annoyance at a notice which reads, "Out to Tea, Joe." He turns away, muttering disgustedly.

30. The following dialogue is somewhat shorter and slightly modified in the film version.

31. JOE is in fact standing at a window, shaving and looking down on the scene below with growing curiosity.

32. In the film, EGBERT sticks a cigarette in one ear and blows smoke out of his nostrils, bringing gasps of amazement from the crowd of admiring small boys.

33. At this point they stop at the door of the Black Pussy Cat.

34. Cut to a close shot of a newspaper: there is a large photograph of Egbert Sousé on the front page, doffing his hat in classic Fields style.

35. Though the preceding sequence is cut in the film, some of the dialogue is included in EGBERT's interview with the REPORTER.

36. EGBERT enters holding the local newspaper which contains the account of his exploits; MRS BRUNCH promptly grabs it from him and hurls it into the fire.

37. EGBERT mounts the stairs, while MRS BRUNCH sucks on her fingers to show that she thinks he is going to smoke in his bedroom. As he starts to mount the stairs, MYRTLE comes dashing headlong down them and collides with her father. She dashes across the room and out on to the porch where she meets OG OGGILBY. She immediately begins to tell her fiancé the story of EGBERT's prowess, a conversation which gradually turns to the sentimental.

38. The preceding sequence, from the meeting between OG and MYRTLE, is cut in the final film version.

39. He jumps with alarm as he sees the coloured man standing just behind him.

40. This speech is cut.

41. EGBERT does not meet OG at this point. Instead, he is first directed by the TELLER to SKINNER's office. He meets OG just outside the door of the office and shakes hands with him there.

42. The whole of the preceding scene, from EGBERT shaking hands with OG outside SKINNER's door, is cut from the finished film version.

43. SKINNER takes the calendar from the drawer of his desk; the

page which shows the nude figure is entitled " Spring in Love ".

44. Minor changes were made to the exchanges between EGBERT and SKINNER in the final film version; EGBERT simpers foolishly throughout the whole conversation.

45. The sequence in which SKINNER presents EGBERT with his uniform is cut in the final version of the film. Instead, EGBERT meets OG on his exit from SKINNER's office. He talks about his new job to OG and promises to come into the bank the next day wearing one of his disguises.

46. EGBERT is in training: he pretends to draw a pistol from the inside of his uniform jacket.

47. Camera cuts backwards and forwards from a shot of EGBERT and WATERBURY together to a close shot of WATERBURY, who is wearing a straw hat and looking a very slippery customer.

48. They both dab their eyes on WATERBURY's handkerchief.

49. There are minor changes to this part of the dialogue in the film version. For instance, EGBERT says at this juncture, " Beer flowing through the estate over your grandmother's paisley shawl."

50. There are frequent cuts throughout this speech from shots of EGBERT and OG together to close shots of each of them alone.

51. EGBERT is very confident and insistent, OG nervous and hesitant.

52. This becomes five hundred dollars in the film.

53. EGBERT tries to look casual, then suddenly jumps on the boy.

54. The LADY first wrenches her son from EGBERT's grasp.

55. The boy makes disparaging remarks about EGBERT's nose, as he is led away by his mother.

56. The bank examiners name is changed to SNOOPINGTON in the film.

57. Throughout this exchange, EGBERT is very effusive, while JOHNSON/SNOOPINGTON looks decidedly uneasy.

58. In the film this incident occurs just as EGBERT is leaving OG.

59. MYRTLE jokes with OG about a word in a crossword puzzle which means " embezzlement ". Another member of the family suggests " prison ". OG looks very sick at this and beckons MYRTLE out on to the porch.

60. MYRTLE also threatens to tell her mother that EGBERT is responsible for OG stealing money from the bank to invest in a beef-steak mine.

61. They halt in front of the entrance to the Black Pussy Cat.

62. JOHNSON/SNOOPINGTON looks very furtive, clearly very much afraid of being recognized.

63. This speech is extended by EGBERT into a long peroration on the delights of the turf.

64. Throughout this exchange, we cut occasionally to JOE, who is looking on blandly from the bar counter.

65. The list of goodies cited by EGBERT is even longer and more nauseating in the film.

66. Room five in the film.

67. This has become a public call box in the hotel lobby in the final film version.

68. EGBERT reaches out towards the exotically decorated hat worn by a woman sitting close by, and appears to pluck some small fruit from it.

69. The following dialogue, until the entrance of EGBERT into JOHNSON/SNOOPINGTON's bedroom, is cut in the final film version.

70. EGBERT breezes in, talking in a very loud voice, which makes JOHNSON/SNOOPINGTON wince.

71. JOHNSON/SNOOPINGTON raises a handkerchief to his mouth, as though about to vomit.

72. He rattles the ping-pong balls four times and holds up four fat fingers.

73. The preceding sequences between EGBERT and HARRIMAN and EGBERT and MYRTLE are cut from the finished version of the film.

74. He tries on a false beard.

75. The STENOGRAPHER is not yet visible.

76. The STENOGRAPHER comes in at this juncture. EGBERT gallantly helps her to a chair, then gazes in fascination at her legs. His attention is finally almost entirely taken by her and he begins to bend amorously towards her.

77. EGBERT does not see him until the bank examiner's name is pronounced, whereupon he spins round with a wild shriek and collides with JOHNSON/SNOOPINGTON.

78. EGBERT squawks with horror outside the door of SKINNER's office, before re-entering the room.

79. EGBERT starts a long and amusing recital of the possible consequences of JOHNSON/SNOOPINGTON's illness.

80. The campaign mounted by EGBERT and OG is almost totally recast in the film. When OG first sees JOHNSON/SNOOPINGTON, he crashes in a dead faint to the floor; a crowd of tellers run to him and flap newspapers over his face to revive him. In the meantime, EGBERT " accidentally " lowers a small metal die-press on to JOHNSON/SNOOPINGTON's hand, and the latter lets out a yelp of pain. OG sits up and then faints again at the sight of the bank examiner. Finally recovering, he joins EGBERT in his campaign to make life difficult for the examiner. EGBERT cuts the cord of JOHNSON/SNOOPINGTON's spectacles, bangs the examiner on the back, thus causing the spectacles to fall on the floor, then promptly treads on them. JOHNSON/SNOOPINGTON does not seem unduly put out by this disaster and merely crosses to his brief-case, which he opens to disclose a seemingly unlimited supply of spare spectacles.

81. After OG's and EGBERT's campaign against the bank examiner, another very important sequence appears in the final film version. We see the crooked WATERBURY sitting in a restaurant reading a newspaper; his face registers terrible shock as he reads of the sudden phenomenal success of the beefsteak mines, the bonds for which he has sold to OG. EGBERT is with OG, when

WATERBURY turns up at the bank and attempts to buy back the bonds from OG. He leaves the two together to finish their business and goes out into the main hall of the bank, just as a newsboy enters. EGBERT promptly grabs a copy of the newspaper from the boy, then reads the news of the beefsteak mine success. EGBERT rushes back into the office where he has left OG and WATERBURY, delivers a straight right to WATERBURY's chin and knocks him through the window. OG thanks EGBERT profusely for saving the valuable bonds which he had been on the point of selling back to WATERBURY.

82. OG is no longer thus obliged to conceal his theft in the film; instead the CROOK obliges him to put his valuable beefsteak bonds into the bag.

83. Cut at this point to OG as he slumps behind the bank counter falling against the burglar alarm and causing it to ring loudly.

84. In the film it is EGBERT who is compelled to drive the car, which he does with crazy panache.

85. The NICODEMUS sequences are cut from the film. Instead there is a sequence of near misses between the DODDS/GREENE car and that driven by EGBERT. There are also frequent cuts to the pursuing police car. At one point, EGBERT's car passes over a trench in which there are a number of workmen wielding pickaxes; one of them catches the underside of the passing car with his axe and is promptly jerked up into the car, only to be ejected immediately by the CROOK.

86. The NICODEMUS scenes are cut from the finished film, as are the preceding explosion and underwear scenes.

87. This chase sequence differs considerably in detail in the finished version of the film. At one point the car occupied by EGBERT and the CROOK comes to a halt on a particularly steep hill. The CROOK orders EGBERT out to push. The car, of course, runs rapidly backwards towards the two pursuing cars. Another shot shows EGBERT and the CROOK speeding down a country lane. EGBERT suddenly tries to brake and we see the brake and clutch pedals collapse through the floor of the car. Then he tries the handbrake, which comes away in his hand. Next the steering wheel comes off in

EGBERT's hands; he turns round and tries to hand it to the now terrified CROOK who is cowering in the back seat. The complete disintegration of the car continues, with little apparent effect on its performance. The last straw for the CROOK, however, comes when one of the wheels starts to part company with the rest of the car, and he tries to jump out. He fails to escape, and when the car finally comes to a halt, the pursuers arrive to find the CROOK lying senseless with fear in the back of the car.

88. There is, of course, no mention of this sum in the film.

89. The following sequence, apart from the presentation of the cheque to EGBERT by DODDS/GREENE, is cut from the final version of the film.

90. This sequence begins with an outside shot of the SOUSE's new residence — a palatial, detached house. At the breakfast table, the whole family is immaculately dressed; a BUTLER waits on them respectfully. EGBERT takes loving leave of his family and, wearing an elegant morning suit, struts away through the hall of the house. His family and MRS BRUNCH gaze admiringly after him. EGBERT continues his pompous progress through the beautifully kept garden, and the film ends as he disappears down the drive. The remainder of the screenplay was not used in the final version of the film.

CONTEMPORARY REVIEWS

No reflection is intended upon the appearance of W. C. Fields when we say that the great man has mellowed considerably, and for the best, since he was last among us in *My Little Chickadee* and, before that, in *You Can't Cheat An Honest Man*. Then he gave signs of degenerating into a pesky, cantankerous old fluff with a disposition as vile as that of a wolverine. But now, in Universal's *The Bank Dick* . . . we welcome our old friend Bill back, as magnificently expansive as ever. . . .

With such a part to play around with, old Bill has the time of his life — growling, feinting, being official and forever preserving his flyblown dignity. No one who fancies madcap comedy can reasonably afford to miss the spectacle of Bill creeping up and pouncing upon a kid with a cap-pistol in the bank; or of Bill solicitously attending a bank examiner whom he has fed a "Michael Finn"; or of Bill at the wheel of the car in which a desperate bandit is attempting to escape. "The resale value of this car," says Bill from the corner of his mouth, "is going to be practically nil when we get through with this trip."

In fact, for anyone who simply likes to laugh at the reckless inanities of an inspired buffoon, we recommend *The Bank Dick*. It's great fun.

BOSLEY CROWTHER,
New York Times

It's a rambling show, part cockeyed fable, part incidental comedy and part just plain W. C. Fields. It's by all odds the funniest show in town. Sense or nonsense, no one can touch Fields in his peculiar type of clowning. . . . If you care for imperishable comedy, don't miss *The Bank Dick*.

HOWARD BARNES,
New York Herald-Tribune